AF608090

THE CATHOLIC UNIVERSITY OF AMERICA
CANON LAW STUDIES
No. 123

PROOF OF DEATH IN PRE-NUPTIAL INVESTIGATION

AN HISTORICAL SYNOPSIS AND COMMENTARY

A DISSERTATION

Submitted to the Faculty of Canon Law of the Catholic University of America in Partial Fulfillment of the Requirements for the Degree of

DOCTOR OF CANON LAW

BY THE

REV. PATRICK W. RICE, A.B., J.C.L.
Priest of the Diocese of Pittsburgh

THE CATHOLIC UNIVERSITY OF AMERICA PRESS
WASHINGTON, D. C.
1940

NIHIL OBSTAT:
HIERONYMUS D. HANNAN, S.T.D., J.C.D.,
Censor Deputatus.
Washingtonii, D. C., die XI Maii, 1940.

IMPRIMATUR:
✠ HUGO C. BOYLE, D.D.,
Episcopus Pittsburgensis.
Pittsburghi, die XI Maii, 1940

PRINTED IN THE UNITED STATES OF AMERICA
BY THE WATKINS PRINTING CO., BALTIMORE

TO MY FATHER

TABLE OF CONTENTS

CHAPTER I. PRELIMINARY NOTIONS

PART ONE — HISTORICAL SYNOPSIS

CHAPTER II. PROOF OF DEATH FROM EARLIEST TIMES TO THE DECRETALS OF GREGORY IX

ARTICLE I. PROOF OF DEATH IN THE EARLY HISTORY OF THE CHURCH 9
A. Roman Law 9
B. The Eastern Church 11
C. The Western Church 12

ARTICLE II. PROOF OF DEATH IN THE PERIOD PRECEDING THE DECRETALS OF GREGORY IX 13
A. The Penitentials 13
B. Councils of Verberies and Compiègne 15
C. Canonical Collections 16
D. Authors 17

CHAPTER III. PROOF OF DEATH FROM THE DECRETALS OF GREGORY IX TO THE PRESENT TIME

ARTICLE I. DECRETALS, COUNCILS, AUTHORS 21
A. The Decretals of Gregory IX 21
B. Canonists 23
C. A pre-Tridentine Council 26
D. The Council of Trent 26
E. Councils and Synods 26
F. Provincial Councils of the Eighteenth and Nineteenth Centuries 28

ARTICLE II. THE SACRED CONGREGATIONS 30

SUMMARY OF HISTORICAL SYNOPSIS 36

PART TWO — CANONICAL COMMENTARY

CHAPTER IV. GENERAL FEATURES OF PROCEDURE IN ESTABLISHING PROOF OF DEATH

Article I. Instruction of the Year 1868 41

Article II. Administrative Procedure 43
A. Administrative Procedure in General 44
B. Administrative Procedure in Proof of Death 50

Article III. Judicial Procedure 51

Article IV. The Pastor's Place in the Investigation .. 54
A. The Pastor's Obligation to Refer the Case to the Ordinary 54
B. In Danger of Death 58

Article V. Proof of Death in Cases Wherein the Missing Person is an Infidel 59

CHAPTER V. PROOF OF DEATH BY DOCUMENTS AND WITNESSES

Article I. Proof by Documents 60

Article II. The Church's Attitude Towards the Civil Declaration of Death 65

Article III. Proof of Death by Witnesses 67
A. Witnesses in General 67
B. Two Eye-witnesses 71
C. One Witness 73
D. Hearsay Witnesses 77
E. The Suppletory Oath 79

CHAPTER VI. PRESUMED DEATH

Article I. Presumptions 81
Article II. Common Opinion 96
Article III. Presumption Cases 98

CHAPTER VII. THE DECLARATION OF DEATH AND ITS LEGAL CONSEQUENCES

Article I. Decision and Recourse 106

A. Moral Certitude 106

B. The Decision 107

C. Recourse 108

Article II. The Impediment of Crime 109

Article III. The Legal Consequences of Erroneous Declaration of Death and the Handling of Doubtful Cases 111

A. Return of a Spouse Thought Dead 111

B. Nullity Cases 114

C. Doubtful Cases 115

CHAPTER VIII. CIVIL LAW PROVISIONS WITH REGARD TO PRESUMED DEATH

Article I. American Civil Law 121

Article II. Continental Civil Law 128

CONCLUSIONS 131

APPENDIX 132

BIBLIOGRAPHY 138

BIOGRAPHICAL NOTE 147

Chapter I

PRELIMINARY NOTIONS

There are several fundamental notions which must be kept in mind in treating the question of proof of death of a previous spouse in view of establishing freedom to contract a second marriage. These are chiefly: the nature of the diriment impediment of a previous bond *(ligamen),* the establishment of freedom to marry *(status liber),* and the lawfulness of entering a second marriage when the first has been dissolved. These will be briefly discussed in this preliminary chapter.

Ligamen [1] is a diriment impediment by which a person who is bound by the bond of a previous marriage cannot validly contract another marriage.[2] In order that the impediment of *ligamen* exist, it is necessary that the first marriage be a valid one, and that it has not been legitimately dissolved.

This impediment is primarily concerned with the unity of marriage, and directly prohibits polygamy.[3] That marriage is essentially monogamous as instituted by the Creator is evidenced by the words of Genesis, "They shall be two in one flesh," [4] words quoted by our Lord when he restored marriage to its primitive dignity. On that occasion he stated that the marriage of Adam and Eve was to be the type and standard of marriage, one and indissoluble.[5] Polyandry, or the simultaneous marriage of one woman with more than one man, is contrary to the primary principles of the natural law.[6] The case is somewhat different with regard to polygamy, or the simultaneous marriage of one man

[1] Rolandus, later Pope Alexander III (d. 1181), seems to have been the first to list *ligamen* as a separate impediment. He used the term *ligatio.*— Thaner, *Summa Magistri Rolandi* (Innsbruck, 1874), *De Coniugio,* p. 114.

[2] Canon 1069, § 1.

[3] Gasparri, *Tractatus Canonicus de Matrimonio* (ed. nova, Romae: Typis Polyglottis Vaticanis, 1932), n. 552; De Smet, *De Sponsalibus et Matrimonio* (4. ed., Brugis: Car. Beyaert, 1927), n. 563.

[4] Genesis, II, 24.

[5] Mark, X, 6-9; Matthew, XIX, 4-6.

[6] De Smet, *De Sponsalibus et Matrimonio,* n. 303.

with several women. The more common opinion of theologians is that polygamy, although not opposed to the primary principles of the natural law, is opposed to the secondary principles of the natural law: but that it was permitted to the Jewish Patriarchs by way of dispensation. As holding this view may be mentioned St. Thomas (d. 1274),[7] Bellarmine (d. 1621)[8] and Billot (d. 1931).[9] Other theologians held that, although polygamy was not opposed to the natural law, it was illicit, because it was forbidden by God. Among those who held this opinion were Durandus a Sancto Porciano (d. 1332),[10] Gerson (d. 1429),[11] and Perrone (d. 1876).[12]

Indirectly the impediment of *ligamen* is concerned with the indissolubility of marriage, for if a person proceeding on the assumption that marriage can be dissolved on account of adultery, desertion, long absence and the like, contracts a further marriage, this second marriage is invalid by reason of the impediment of *ligamen*. The doctrine of the indissolubility of marriage, received by the Church from her divine founder and defended by her against the attacks of heretics and secular powers throughout the ages, was affirmed dogmatically by the Council of Trent.[13] The

[7] *Commentum in IV Libros Sententiarum*, lib. IV, d. XXXIII, q. 1, art. 2—*Opera Omnia* (Parmae, 1856), Vol. VII; *Summa Theol.*, Suppl., q. 65, a. 2.

[8] *De Sacramento Matrimonii*, lib. I, c. 11—*Opera Omnia* (Venetiis, 1721), Vol. III.

[9] *De Ecclesiae Sacramentis* (Romae, 1891), II, 374.

[10] *In Petri Lombardi Sententias Theologicas Commentariorum Libri IV* (Venetiis, 1586), lib. IV, d. XXXIII, q. 1.

[11] *Opera Omnia* (Antwerp, 1706), Tom. III, *Regulae Morales*, Regula CXLVII.

[12] *De Matrimonio Christiano* (Romae, 1858), III, 34.

[13] "Si quis dixerit, Ecclesiam errare, cum docuit et docet, iuxta evangelium et apostolicam doctrinam, propter adulterium alterius coniugum matrimonii vinculum non posse dissolvi, et utrumque, vel etiam innocentem, qui causam adulterio non dedit, non posse, altero coniuge vivente, aliud matrimonium contrahere, moecharique, qui dimissa adultera aliam duxerit, et eam, qui dimisso adultero alii nupserit: anathema sit."—Conc. Trident., sess. XXIV, *de matrimonio*, canon 7—Denzinger-Bannwart, *Enchiridion*, n. 977. The indirect wording of this canon was adopted by the Council of Trent to avoid antagonizing the Greek Catholics. Cf. Palla-

direct object of the dogma is that the Church does not err in its teaching concerning the indissolubility of the marriage bond; the indirect object is the indissolubility of marriage.[14]

The bond of marriage can be dissolved in three ways. These are:

1. Dissolution of the *matrimonium ratum et non consummatum* either a) by papal dispensation, or b) by solemn religious profession.[15]

2. The *privilegium fidei,* including the Pauline privilege.[16]

3. The death of one of the parties. A consummated marriage between baptized persons is dissolved only by death.[17]

If a person has been already married, he cannot contract a second marriage until it has been proved legitimately and certainly that the first marriage is no longer in existence, either through dissolution or nullity of the first marriage.[18] For marriage enjoys the favor of law. Wherefore, in case of doubt the validity of a marriage must be upheld until the contrary is proved, taking into account, however, the ruling of canon 1127.[19] When a ratified but unconsummated marriage has been dissolved, or when a marriage has been dissolved *in favorem fidei,* the fact must be proved by authentic documents from the competent ecclesiastical authorities. If a marriage has been dissolved by death, and authentic documentary proof is not available, a declaration of death must be obtained from the Ordinary in accordance with the Instruction of 1868. With regard to the nullity of the first marriage, a private conviction of this fact does not suffice, but the matter must have been handled, and the fact established by the competent ecclesiastical tribunals.[20]

vicino, *Vera Concilii Tridentini Historia* (Antwerp, 1670), lib. XXII, c. 4, nn. 27-30.

[14] Palmieri, *De Matrimonio Christiano* (Romae, 1880), p. 142; Perrone, *De Matrimonio Christiano,* III, 415.

[15] Canon 1119.

[16] Canon 1120.

[17] Canon 1118.

[18] Canon 1069, § 2.

[19] Canon 1014.

[20] Canons 1987-1990.

The investigation preliminary to marriage, especially to discover the existence of any impediments to marriage, devolves upon the pastor. It is his obligation to question the parties who are to be married with regard to the possibility of a previous marriage on the part of one or both.[21] If the dissolution or nullity of a previous marriage is not demonstrated by authentic documents, he may not proceed with the marriage, but must present the case to the Ordinary. In these days when the sanctity and indissolubility of marriage are so little regarded outside the Catholic Church, the pastor should be especially careful when assisting at mixed marriages to make sure that the non-Catholic party has not been previously married.

When it has been demonstrated with certainty and according to law that a previous marriage has been dissolved, a new marriage is permitted. While there have been a number of heresies which considered second marriages invalid, the Catholic Church has always held that they were both valid and licit.[22] There have been individual writers, including some of the Fathers, who went to extremes in expressing their disapproval of second marriages; but the official attitude of the Church has been that, although it is better for a person not to marry again, if he wishes to contract a second marriage after the dissolution of the first, it is permitted.[23] This traditional view of the Church is still in force today.[24]

Granted that marriage is dissolved by death, it is not always easy to prove that one of the parties to a marriage has died, and

[21] Canons 1019, 1020 and 1030.

[22] Innocent III, ep. *"Eius exemplo"*, 18 dec. 1208, (profession of faith prescribed for the Waldenses who wished to be reconciled to the Church) —Denzinger-Bannwart, *Enchiridion,* n. 424; Innocent IV, *Ep.* 10, *ad Ottonem Card. Tusculanum,* n. 20—Mansi, XXIII, 581; Profession of faith accepted by the Emperor Michael Palaeologus previous to the Council of Lyons in 1274—Denzinger-Bannwart, *Enchiridion,* n. 465; Benedict XIV, const. *"Etsi Pastoralis"*, 26 maii 1742, § VIII, n. 3—*Fontes,* n. 328.

[23] Sanchez, *De Sancto Matrimonii Sacramento* (Antwerp, 1626), lib. VII, disp. 81.

[24] Canon 1142.

thus to establish the freedom of the other to marry again. This has been a knotty problem since the earliest days of the Church. Wars, captivity, shipwrecks, earthquakes and similar disasters have always resulted in the disappearance of individuals without absolute proof of their death being available. In past ages the slowness of transportation and the uncertainty and delay in communication between distant points were factors which made the proof of death often difficult to obtain. It may be said that the increase in means and the improvement in methods of communications have made it easier in modern times to obtain certainty of the death of a missing person.

Nevertheless new factors have arisen in modern times to complicate the problem, for example, the emigration of so many Europeans to other countries. Rapid transportation has given rise to new problems with regard to the proof of death of an absent spouse, especially in the United States, where people think so little of travelling long distances and settling far from their original homes. The frequency of civil divorce in our age is another factor. When the parties to a marriage obtain a civil divorce, they tend to lose track of each other, and in the course of time they are frequently entirely unaware of the whereabouts of the other party; thus they often do not know whether their former spouse is alive or dead.

In the succeeding chapters, the history of this problem in ecclesiastical legislation will first be traced, and then the process for proof of death in accordance with present ecclesiastical legislation will be discussed.

PART ONE

HISTORICAL SYNOPSIS

Chapter II

PROOF OF DEATH FROM EARLIEST TIMES TO THE DECRETALS OF GREGORY IX

Article I. Proof of Death in the Early History of the Church

A. *Roman Law*

Roman Law is of great importance in this question, as its provisions governing the proof of death in marriage cases conflicted in certain points with the laws of the Church, and throughout the centuries the civil authorities continued to make use of Justinian's provisions in settling the difficulties that arose in the matter.

There is one passage in the Digest which refers to the proof of death of an absent spouse. The case is as follows: A woman hearing that her absent husband had died married again. Shortly thereafter the absent husband returned. The jurist asks what should be done to the woman. His solution is that, if a long time had passed and it was clear that she had been deceived by false rumors of his death, her second marriage should be considered legitimate.[1] Romanists are undecided as to whether this passage indicates that long absence dissolved marriage in the classical period, or whether this is a case of reasonable presumption of death, making the second marriage legitimate.[2]

That marriage was dissolved in the classical period by captivity is evident from a number of texts.[3] There is one text in the Digest which declares that, if a man falls into the hands of the enemy, his wife must wait five years before contracting a second marriage, unless she has obtained certain evidence of his death.[4] However, it is practically certain that this passage was interpolated by the codifiers of Justinian; it therefore reflects Justinian,

[1] D. (48.5) 12.12.

1930), p. 215.

[2] Corbett, *The Roman Law of Marriage* (Oxford: Clarendon Press,

[3] D. (24.2) 1; D. (49.15) 8; D. (49.15) 12.4; D. (49.15) 14.

[4] D. (24.2) 6.

and not classical, law.[5] The only exception, in classical law, to the general rule on captivity was the case in which a patron, married to his freed-woman, was captured by the enemy. The jurists disagreed as to whether the marriage in thise case still continued or was dissolved.[6]

Justinian, however, changed the law concerning the dissolution of the marriage bond through captivity. He decreed that captivity no longer dissolved marriage; that, where it was uncertain whether the person captured was alive or dead, the other spouse was to wait five years before contracting a new marriage.[7]

There are three constitutions in post-classical Roman Law which refer to the question of proof of death with regard to soldiers away on military expeditions, concerning whom nothing has been heard for some time. According to a constitution of Constantine in 337, a woman who had received no news concerning her husband, away on military service, for four years, could contract another marriage, provided that she communicated with her husband's commander and informed him of her intention to remarry.[8] Justinian in 536 changed the period of waiting to ten years, and also required the wife to make an effort to locate her husband by getting in touch with the military officials under whom he had served.[9] Finally in 542 Justinian decreed that a wife in these circumstances could not remarry no matter how long her husband had been absent. She could marry only if she received the sworn testimony of the military commander that her husband was dead. Even after this testimony was received she had to wait a year before proceeding to another marriage.[10]

[5] Corbett, *The Roman Law of Marriage,* p. 212.

[6] D. (23.2) 45.

[7] "Quodsi incertum sit, utrum quae ad hostes pervenit persona supersit necne, tunc quinquennium expectandum est sive marito sive uxore, quo peracto, sive de morte explorata fuerit res sive incerta maneat, sine periculo matrimonium inire licet."—N. (22.7). This was reaffirmed in N. (117.12).

[8] C. (5.17) 7.

[9] N. (22.14).

[10] N. (117.11).

To sum up, the Roman Law as it crystallized under Justinian decreed that in cases of long absence a person could not contract another marriage unless the death of the other spouse was proved by documentary evidence, with the exception, however, that in cases of captivity the other party could proceed to a new marriage after five years, if it was uncertain whether the person taken captive was alive or dead.[11]

B. *The Eastern Church*

St. Basil in a letter to Amphilochius (374) has two canons which refer to remarriage when one of the spouses has been absent without news. Canon 31 states that a woman is guilty of adultery if she remarries without obtaining certitude of the death of her absent husband.[12] In canon 36 Basil states that the wives of soldiers are to be governed by the same regulations as apply in the previous canon. However, he admits that their remarrying in this case is less reprehensible, as the presumption of death is greater.[13]

The Council of Trullo (692), which is very authoritative in the canon law of the Greek Church, repeats the canons of Basil, but in addition declares that when a soldier returns after a long

[11] The Emperor Leo the Philosopher (886-912), towards the close of the ninth century, in his 33rd Novel changed the 117th Novel of Justinian with regard to captivity by requiring certainty of death in this case also before remarriage would be permitted. This provision affected the civil law of the Eastern Empire. It does not seem to have carried much weight even in the East, for as a matter of fact the Nomocanon of Photius (883), the basic canon law of the Eastern Church, still carries the legislation of Justinian on the matter. Nomocanon, XIII, c. 4.—Pitra *Ius Ecclesiasticum Graecorum* (Romae, 1864-1868), II, 614.

[12] "Cuius vir discessit, nec comparet, ea antequam de eius morte certior facta sit, una cum alio habitans moechatur." *Ep. 199, ad Amphilochium,* canon 31—*MPL,* XXXII, 727.

[13] "Militum uxores, quae maritis suis non comparentibus, nupserunt, rationi eidem subiiciuntur, cui et illae, quae ob peregrinationem maritorum reditum non expectavere: sed tamen res nonnullam hic veniam admittit, quod maior sit mortis suspicio." *Ep. 199, ad Amphilochium,* canon 36—*MPL,* XXXII, 727.

absence and finds that his wife has married again, he may take her back if he wishes.[14]

C. *The Western Church*

Two papal documents of great importance in this matter are the decretal letters of Pope Innocent I (401-417) to Probus and of Pope St. Leo I (440-461) to Nicetas.

In the Gothic invasion of 410 Ursa, the wife of Fortunius, was taken a prisoner by the barbarians. In the course of time Fortunius married again. Ursa later obtained her freedom from her captors, and on her return brought the case to the attention of the Pope, Innocent I. The Pope's decision was that the first marriage was established by divine grace, and that the second marriage had no claim to legality.[15]

The letter of St. Leo dealt with similar cases which arose as a result of the invasion of Italy by Attila in 452, in the course of which many people were killed and others carried into captivity. In many of these cases the wives of the missing men, presuming the deaths of their consorts, had entered into new marriages. However, some of the missing individuals returned, and naturally difficulties arose. Nicetas, Bishop of Aquileia, wrote to the Pope and asked what procedure should be followed. St. Leo declared that since the first marriages were legitimate, the second marriages must be broken off, and the parties of the first marriages must be reunited. In any instances where the wives would refuse to break off the second unions and return to the first they were to be excommunicated.[16]

These two decretals exerted a very great influence in the West. They established the principle that marriage is not dissolved by any absence or by a mere presumption of death on the part of one of the spouses. Thus they implicitly demanded proof of death before a new marriage could be contracted. The letter of St. Leo is certainly the classical document on the question up to

[14] Canon 93—Mansi, XI, 982.

[15] *Ep. 26 Probo—MPL,* XX, 602; Jaffé, *Regesta,* n. 313.

[16] *Ep. 159, ad Nicetam—Bullarium Romanum* (Augustae Taurinorum, 1857-1872), n. XVIII, I, 78; *MPL,* LIV, 1135.

the time of the Decretals of Gregory IX. Both letters received a large circulation and were well known due to their being included in two of the most important canonical collections of the early period. They are both to be found in the *Collectio Dionysiana,*[17] compiled by Dionysius Exiguus at the beginning of the sixth century, which was widely diffused in France, Spain, Africa, England, and even in the Orient, and which had a very great influence upon later collections in the Western Church.[18] These two decretals are also found in another important collection of the period, which had great authority in Spain, the *Collectio Isidoriana,* sometimes called the *Later Hispana.*[19]

Article II. Proof of Death in the Period Preceding the Decretals of Gregory IX

A. *The Penitentials*

In the breakdown of discipline which characterized the Frankish Church from the seventh to the ninth centuries, great laxity was shown in permitting a person to remarry when his or her spouse was taken into captivity. Largely responsible for this abuse, and others in connection with the indissolubility of the marrage bond, was the circulation in the Frankish kingdom of the *Penitential of Theodore* and other similar works. Penitentials were books used by the ordinary priests in their ministry, which guided them especially in the administering of penances for sin, but which also contained other matters. Penitentials seem to have arisen in Ireland, and then spread to England and later to France.[20]

[17] *Collectio Decretorum Pontificum Romanorum,* c. 37 (Innocent to Probus)—*MPL,* LXVII, 251; cc. 42-45 (Leo to Nicetas)—*MPL,* LXVII, 296.

[18] Maassen, *Geschichte der Quellen und der Literatur des canonischen Rechts* (Gratz, 1870), nn. 580-585.

[19] *Epistolae Decretales,* n. 14 (Innocent to Probus)—*MPL,* LXXXIV, 655; n. 68 (Leo to Nicetas)—*MPL,* LXXXIV, 774.

[20] Paul Fournier, "Etudes sur les Penitentiels"—*Revue d'Histoire et de le Litterature Religieuses,* IX (1904), 102. It is noteworthy that the first two penitentials of which there is record (both Irish works), that of *Finnian* of the sixth century (McNeill-Gamer, *Medieval Handbooks of*

The *Penitential of Theodore,*[21] which had a great circulation in the Frankish kingdom was especially lax in this matter. It permitted a husband or wife to remarry after one year, if the other spouse was taken captive by force and redemption was impossible. Where redemption was possible, remarriage was permitted after five years.[22] Similar provisions are found in other penitentials of this period.[23] The Council of Chalons in 813 [24] and the Council of Paris in 829 [25] took steps to do away with the use of penitentials. The former told the clergy to disregard them, and to follow instead the canons. The latter commanded that penitentials which were found to differ from the canons should be confiscated and burned.

Since penitentials of some kind were necessary for priests,

Penance, Records of Civilization: Sources and Studies, Columbia University, XXIX [New York: Columbia University Press, 1938], pp. 95-96) and the *Penitential of Cummean* (Zettinger, "Das Poenitentiale Cummeani,"—*AKKR,* LXXXII [1902], 502-503) do not contain any of the lax provisions which are to be found in later penitentials with regard to the remarriage of those whose spouses had been taken into captivity. This is strong evidence of the practice of the Irish Church of this period in the matter.

[21] Theodore, a Greek, was sent to England in 668 by Pope Vitalian, as Archbishop of Canterbury, and was entrusted with the mission of safeguarding faith and morals in the English Church. That he was the author of the Penitential bearing his name seems unlikely (Fournier-Le Bras, *Histoire des Collections Canoniques en Occident* [Paris: Recueil Sirey, 1931], I, 54); everything points to his great loyalty to the teachings of the Church, and as a matter of fact he presided at the Council of Hertford (673), in which the provisions concerning marriage are all in harmony with the teachings of the Church (Canon 10—Mansi, XI, 130).

[22] Lib. II, c. 12, § 20-24—Haddan and Stubbs, *Councils and Ecclesiastical Documents relating to Great Britain and Ireland* (Oxford, 1869-1873), III, 200-201.

[23] *Poenitentiale Bedae* (remarriage permitted after the lapse of one year), "De Usuris"—Mansi, XII, 512; *Excerptiones Egberti* (remarriage permitted after seven years' absence), n. 123—*MPL,* LXXXIX, 393: *Poenitentiale Egberti* (remarriage permitted after waiting for six years), lib. I, c. 26—*MPL,* LXXXIX, 408.

[24] Canon 38—Mansi, XIV, 101.

[25] Lib. I, canon 32—Mansi, XIV, 559.

several were composed at this period which were based on the approved canons. In these penitentials there is no trace of anything contrary to the teaching of the Church on the question of the remarriage of those whose spouses were in captivity.[26] Nevertheless, the old penitentials still seem to have had a certain circulation for a time, and thereby helped to promote a lax practice on this question and others pertaining to marriage.[27]

B. *Councils of Verberies and Compiègne*

The ease with which a second marriage was permitted in France in the eighth century in case of long absence of one of the spouses is evident from canons of the Councils or rather Capitularies[28] of Verberies and Compiègne. The Council of Verberies (Vernon-sur-Seine) in 756[29] dealt with the case of a man who was forced to leave his native land and to live permanently elsewhere. It permitted him to remarry, if his wife refused to accompany him into exile; she, however, was not permitted to remarry so long as he lived.[30] The Council of Compiègne (757) did not permit remarriage in the case wherein a person was forced to leave the country; instead, it decreed that neither the husband nor the wife could remarry in this case.[31] However, in a decision handed down in a particular case the Council relaxed this strict rule by permitting a man, who had left his wife in a foreign country, to retain as his wife the woman whom he married on returning to his native land.[32] These two

[26] E.g., Hatto of Basel, *Capitulare—MPL,* CV, 766; Rhabanus Maurus, *Liber Paenitentium—MPL,* CXII, 1406; *Paenitentiale—MPL,* CX, 488; Halitgarus, *De Paenitentia,* lib. IV—*MPL,* CV, 682.

[27] Paul Fournier, "Études sur Les Peniteniels,"—*Revue d'Histoire et de Littérature Réligieuses,* VIII (1903), 551.

[28] Since the laity took part in these synods, they are rather royal capitularies than ecclesiastical councils.

[29] The name and date of this council are here given as quoted by Joyce, *Christian Marriage* (Heythrop Theological Series, I, London: Sheed and Ward, 1933), p. 342.

[30] C. 9—Mansi, XVII B, 164; *MGH, Leges,* Sect. II, 41.

[31] C. 21—*MGH, Leges,* Sect. II, 39; c. 18— Mansi, XVII B, 184.

[32] C. 9—*MGH, Leges,* Sect. II, 38; c. 6—Mansi, XVII B, 182.

assemblies did a great deal of harm, as they found their way into two important collections of canon law, that of Regino of Prüm and the one of Burchard of Worms.[33]

The reform of marriage discipline in the French Church, begun by the circulation of the *Collectio Dionysio-Hadriana* at the beginning of the ninth century,[34] culminated in the Council of Rouen (1072). A canon of this council is notable for two reasons: it specifically requires certitude of the death of a spouse, before a person can contract a new marriage; and it calls for the imposition of the penalty of excommunication on those who disregard this rule.[35]

C. *Canonical Collections*

The spurious collection of Benedict the Levite (847) contains the strict canon (canon 21) of the Council of Compiègne.[36] Regino of Prüm (906), although quoting the lax canons of Verberies (canon 9) and Compiègne (canon 9),[37] also quotes the decretal of Pope St. Leo I to Nicetas.[38] Canon 9 of the Council of Verberies appears again in the collection of Burchard of Worms (circa 1020),[39] but the letter of Pope St. Leo I is also given.[40] The classical decretal of Pope St. Leo I is also quoted in the

[33] Cf. *infra*, p. 16.

[34] Under Charlemagne a real reform took place in the Frankish Church with regard to marriage legislation. Pope Adrian I in 774 sent to Charlemagne a copy of the collection of Canons by Dionysius Exiguus, which contained, as has been seen (*supra*, p. 15), the decretals of Pope Innocent I to Probus and of Pope St. Leo I to Nicetas. This collection with additions by the Pope is called the *Dionysio-Hadriana*, and at the instance of the Emperor was received and approved by the bishops of the Empire at Aix-La-Chapelle in 802 as the *Ancient Code of the Canons of the Roman Church*—Maassen, *Geschichte der Quellen*, n. 588.

[35] Canon 18: "Item si uxor viri, qui peregre aut alias profectus fuerit, alii vero nupserit, quousque prioris mortis ceritudinem habeat, excommunicetur usque ad dignam satisfactionem."—Mansi, XX, 39.

[36] *Capitularium Collectio*, lib. I, c. 8—*MGH, Leges*, II, pars altera, 47.

[37] *De Ecclesiastica Disciplina*, lib. II, cc. 124, 127—*MPL*, CXXXII, 308.

[38] *Op. cit.*, lib. II, cc. 182-183—*MPL*, CXXXII, 319.

[39] *Decretum*, lib. IX, c. 54—*MPL*, CXL, 824.

[40] *Decretum*, lib. IX, cc. 55-58—*MPL*, CXL, 824.

Collectio LXXIV Titulorum (1050),[41] and in the collection of Anselm of Lucca (1080),[42] and both the decretals of Innocent I and St. Leo I are to be found in a collection recorded in a twelfth century manuscript at the Vatican.[43] In the collections of Ivo of Chartres (late eleventh century) the letters of Innocent[44] and St. Leo[45] are also found. In addition, Ivo quotes the ninth canon of Verberies, but by omitting the last sentence makes it a strict prohibition of remarriage before the death of an absent spouse has been ascertained.[46] Finally Ivo quotes a passage from the interpolated passage in the Digest,[47] which states that a woman may not proceed to a new marriage, as long as it is certain that her husband still lives in captivity.[48]

Gratian is perfectly orthodox in his treatment of the question, including in his collection only such canons as illustrate the traditional attitude of the Church on the proof of death of an absent spouse. He quotes the decretals of Innocent and Leo, and the ninth canon of Verberies in the same fashion as Ivo quoted it.[49]

D. *Authors*

Hugh of St. Victor (d. 1141) quotes the letter of Pope St. Leo

[41] Tit. LXIII, c. 272—Fahrner, *Geschichte der Ehescheidung im kanonischen Recht* (Freiburg im Breisgau, 1903), p. 110.

[42] Lib. X, c. 22—Thaner, *Anselmi Episcopi Lucensis Collectio Canonum* (Innsbruck, 1906-1915), p. 492.

[43] Fahrner, *op. cit.*, p. 112.

[44] *Decretum,* pars VIII, c. 245—*MPL,* CLXI, 638; *Panormia,* lib. VI, c. 89—*MPL,* CLXI, 1264.

[45] *Decretum,* pars VIII, cc. 190-194, 244—*MPL,* CLXI, 624, 637; *Panormia,* lib. VI, cc. 86-88—*MPL,* CLXI, 1263.

[46] "Si quis necessitate inevitabili cogente, in alium ducatum seu provinciam fugerit, et uxor eius cum valet et potest amore parentum aut rerum suarum eum sequi noluerit, ipsa omni tempore, quamdiu vir eius quem secuta non fuit, vivit, semper innupta permaneat."—*Decretum,* pars. VIII, c. 189—*MPL,* CLXI, 623; *Panormia,* lib. VI, c. 91—*MPL,* CLXI, 1264.

[47] D. (24. 2) 6. Cf. *supra,* p. 9.

[48] "Generaliter definiendum est, donec certum est maritum vivere in captivitate constitutum, nullam habere licentiam uxores eorum migrare ad aliud matrimonium."—*Decretum,* pars VIII, c. 246—*MPL,* CLXI, 638.

[49] Cc. 1, 2, 4, C. XXXIV, q. 1 and 2. Cf. also c. 2, C. XXXV, q. 9.

I in his writings. He refers also to the case of a man living in a foreign country and marrying a woman who is unaware that he is already married. Hugh calls such a man *criminalis,* although he excuses the woman in the case on account of ignorance; but he stresses the fact that their union is no marriage.[50] The doctrine of Peter Lombard is likewise orthodox. He quotes both the letter of Leo and canon 21 of Compiègne.[51] However, Lombard gave an erroneous solution of a particular case. It concerned a man who left his wife and then went into a foreign country, and there remarried. Lombard would permit the man, if constrained by circumstances, to live with the woman, to continue marriage relations, not indeed at his, but at her request.[52]

St. Thomas Aquinas corrected this as a false solution of the cases, and it obtained no further circulation.[53] St. Thomas states that a woman may proceed to another marriage when her husband has long been absent, but only when she has obtained certitude of his death.[54]

The Decretists followed the traditional teaching in this matter. Rufinus (1165), while strict in principle, is less exacting than later writers in the proof that he would demand for the death of an absent spouse. He would permit remarriage after the lapse of a year where uncertainty existed as to the death of a spouse, provided that there were strong presumptions for believing that

[50] *Summa Sententiarum,* tract. VIII, c. 9—*MPL,* CLXXVI, 161.

[51] *Libri IV Sententiarum,* lib. IV, d. XXXVIII, c. 3—Ed. studio et cura PP. Collegii S. Bonaventurae (ad Claras Aquas [Quaracchi], 1916), II, 970-972.

[52] "Sed ex quo, ad primam redire volens non valens, cogitur Ecclesiae disciplina hanc tenere, incipit excusari per obedientiam et timorem de hoc, quod poscenti mulieri debitum reddit, a qua ipse nunquam poscere debet. Et sic de aliis huiusmodi sentiendum est."—*Ibidem.*

[53] "Hic magister falsum dicit: quia potius debet excommunicatus mori, quam coniungatur illi quae non est sua uxor; hoc enim esset contra veritatem vitae, quae non est propter scandalum dimittenda."—*Commentum in Lib. IV Sententiarum,* lib. IV, d. XXXVIII, Expositio textus.

[54] " . . . non ex levi praesumptione, sed ex aliquo certo iudicio habito de morte viri."—*Ibidem.*

the party in question was dead.[55] Like Roland Bandinelli and other proponents of the *copula* theory,[56] Rufinus held that a long period of captivity dissolved an unconsummated marriage.[57]

Roland Bandinelli, later Pope Alexander III, demanded an adequate proof *(probatio competens)* for the death of a spouse before permitting a new marriage, but did not amplify this statement.[58] Roland likewise considered that captivity dissolved an unconsummated marriage, and in the case where a spouse

55 "Si vero ignoraverit et violentis praesumptionibus fides sibi facta fuerit, poterit post annum sine peccato alterum accipere; si aliter egerit, adultera erit."—In cc. 1, 2, C. XXXIV, q. 1 and 2—Singer, *Summa Decretorum Magistri Rufini* (Paderborn, 1902), p. 507. Referring to the statement of St. Augustine, that he is an adulterer who marries again when his wife is absent for a long time, Rufinus says: "Sed illud, quando maritus vel uxor scitur adhuc vivere; istud, quando *certis indiciis* putatur mortuus esse."—*Ibidem.* In another passage he makes the statement: " . . . ut in nullo casu aliquis vivente uxore sua, cum qua una caro effectus est, aliam possit accipere, nisi cum longe et diu absente uxore ignorat eam vivere, ut dicitur infra [C. XXXIV, q. 1 and 2]."—ed. Singer, p. 492.

56 In the twelfth century there arose a controversy between the school of Bologna and the school of Paris with regard to the canonical effect of marital consent. The former claimed that the consent of the parties gave rise only to a *matrimonium initiatum,* and that the marriage did not become sacramental and indissoluble until it was consummated (*copula* theory) (Cf. Wernz-Vidal, *Ius Canonicum,* V, n. 243). Gratian was in favor of this view (Dictum ad c. 28, C. XXVII, q. 2; c. 16, C. XXVII, q. 2; dictum ad c. 45, C. XXVII, q. 2). The school of Paris held that consent made the marriage sacramental and indissoluble. Peter Lombard was the main spokesman for this view (*Libri IV Sententiarum,* lib. IV, d. XXVII, cc. 3-10). The question was finally settled by Pope Alexander III, who as Rolandus at the school of Bologna had held the *copula* theory (*Summa Magistri Rolandi,* C. XXVII, q. 2—ed. Thaner, pp. 126-132). As Pope, however, he decided that consent effected marriage, but that until the marriage was consummated the bond was capable of dissolution by ecclesiastical authority (C. 7, X, *de conversione coniugatorum,* III, 32).

57 In C. XXVII, q. 2—ed. Singer, p. 443.

58 "Tunc non dicitur vir ei vivere, quando competenti probatione admota ipsum credit obiise. Si qua ergo competenti fide sibi facta credens virum suum obiise alteri nubit, quousque virum suum vivere ignoraverit, immunis erit." *Summa Rolandi,* C. XXXIV—ed. Thaner, p. 200.

returned after a long captivity to find that the other party had remarried, Roland would consider the second marriage valid if the first marriage was unconsummated *(matrimonium initiatum)*.[59] It should be kept in mind that as Pope Alexander III, Roland discarded the *copula* theory altogether, and decided that consent makes marriage. As Pope, therefore, he no longer held that captivity dissolved an unconsummated marriage.

[59] *Ibidem.*

Chapter III

PROOF OF DEATH FROM THE DECRETALS OF GREGORY IX TO THE PRESENT TIME

Article I. Decretals, Councils, Authors

A. *The Decretals of Gregory IX*

The Decretals of Gregory IX, published in 1234, contained two important papal decrees concerning the proof of death of an absent spouse. Both of these decrees were written on the occasion of the wars then waging between the Spaniards and the Saracens. Many Christians were taken prisoners by the Saracens, families were separated, and it was usually impossible for those who were made prisoners to find out what had happened to their husbands and wives. It was equally difficult for those who had escaped the onrush of the Saracens to know whether their spouses were killed in the war or taken captive.

The matter was brought to the attention of Pope Lucius III (1181-1185), who wrote a letter addressed to all Christians held in captivity by the Saracens. He forbade any of them to contract a new marriage until they had certain proof that the party to their first marriage was dead.[1] In cases where individuals had already married without keeping this rule, and doubt still existed concerning the death of the first spouse, the *debitum coniugale* might be given if requested, but could not be demanded. In such cases, if it becomes evident that the first spouse was in reality alive, the parties to the second marriage had to be separated, and the first union restored.[2]

The letter of Clement III (1188) to the Bishop of Saragossa

[1] " . . . id vobis auctoritate apostolica respondemus, ut nullus ex vobis amodo ad secundas nuptias migrare praesumat, donec ei firma certitudine constet, quod ab hac vita migraverit coniux eius."—C. 2, X, *de secundis nuptiis,* IV, 21.

[2] This letter was published previously in the first (edited by Bernard of Pavia, some time between 1181 and 1192) of the *Quinque Compilationes Antiquae.* Cf. Compilatio I, lib. IV, tit. 22, c. 3—Friedberg, *Quinque Compilationes Antiquae* (Leipzig, 1882), p. 53.

is much more specific than the letter of Lucius III. It is certainly the most important document on the question of proof of death of a missing spouse since the letter of St. Leo I, over seven hundred years before. The Bishop had presented to the Pope the problem of some women in his diocese, whose husbands by reason of captivity or a long journey had been absent for over seven years. Although diligent efforts had been made it was impossible to decide whether the men were living or dead. The women were young, and were desirous of marrying again. The Pope, basing his decision on the words of St. Paul: "A woman is bound by the law as long as her husband liveth:", I. Cor., vii, 39, answered that the passage of time has nothing to do with the matter; as long as their husbands live they cannot canonically marry again. The Bishop was forbidden to permit them to remarry with the authority of the Church, until they had received a *certum nuncium* of the death of their husbands.[3]

The importance of these two letters cannot be overestimated, for the Decretals of Gregory IX had the force of universal law up to the publication of the present Code. Therefore these two decretals were the law of the Church on the question of proof of death of an absent spouse.

There are two decretals which caused some difficulty with regard to this question. The first is a decretal of Innocent III (1198-1216) in which the phrase occurs: "Tamdiu alteruter coniugum expectetur, donec de ipsius obitu verisimiliter praesumatur."[4] However, this decretal must be understood in connection with the decretal of Clement III, so that the presumption is founded on a *certum nuncium* or other equivalent proofs.[5]

[3] "Respondemus, quod quantocunque annorum numero ita remaneant, viventibus viris suis non possunt ad aliorum consortium canonice convolare, nec tu eas auctoritate ecclesiae permittas contrahere, donec certum nuncium recipiant de morte virorum."—C. 19, X, *de sponsalibus et matrimoniis,* IV, 1. This decretal was published previously in the second (compiled by John of Wales between 1210 and 1215) of the *Quinque Compilationes Antiquae.* Cf. Comp. II, lib. IV, tit. 1, c. 3—ed. Friedberg, p. 91.

[4] C. 5, X, *ut lite non contestata non procedatur ad testium receptionem vel ad sententiam diffinitivam,* II, 6.

[5] Sanchez, *De Sancto Matrimonii Sacramento,* lib. II, disp. 46, n. 9.

The other is a decretal of Alexander III, issued in 1170 or 1171. The following case was presented to the Pope. It was alleged that the bishop of a certain diocese had granted a divorce with permission to remarry to a woman whose husband was absent in a foreign country for more than ten years. The question then arose in connection with an inheritance: were the children of this second union legitimate? The Pope expressed a doubt that the bishop had done such a thing, but if it was found on further investigation that he had, the children were to be declared legitimate, as born of a putative marriage.[6]

Whatever the facts are concerning the action of the bishop, it is clear from the document that Alexander by no means approved of the divorce on account of long absence but merely responded to the question raised as to the legitimacy of the children.[7]

B. *Canonists*

The practically unanimous opinion of canonists always was that the Roman Law provisions with regard to the proof of death of an absent spouse had no standing in canon law.[8]

Until the Holy Office by its decrees in the course of time settled the doubts, there were three important questions relative to the proof of death of a husband or wife to engage the canonists in disputed discussions. The first question was whether moral certitude was required of the death of a spouse before proceeding to another marriage, or whether moral probability would suffice. Most canonists held that moral certitude was required.[9] The most important canonist who held that moral probability would suffice

[6] C. 8, X, *qui filii sint legitimi,* IV, 17.

[7] Giraldi, *Expositio Iuris Pontificii* (Romae, 1830), II, Sectio 728.

[8] Cf. Sanchez, *De Sancto Matrimonii Sacramento,* lib. II, disp. 46, nn. 1-2. Rufinus would seem to hold to Roman Law provisions in requiring a year's delay on the part of the woman.—Cf. *supra,* p. 18.

[9] Abbas Antiquus, glossa to c. 19, X, *de sponsalibus et matrimoniis,* IV, 1; Panormitanus, in c. 19, X, *de sponsalibus et matrimoniis,* IV, 1; Covarruvias, *De Matrimonio* (Genevae, 1762), pars II, c. 7, § 3, n. 3; Sanchez, *De Sancto Matrimonii Sacramento,* lib. II, disp. 46, nn. 6-9; Pirhing, lib. IV, tit. 1, § 5, n. 2; Schmalzgrueber, lib. IV, tit. 21, n. 5; Reiffenstuel lib. IV, tit. 21, n. 7.

for the proof of death of a spouse was Hostiensis. He based his opinion on the passage in c. 5, X, *ut lite non contestata non procedatur ad testium receptionem vel ad sententiam diffinitivam,* II, 6: "Tamdiu alteruter coniugum expectetur, donec de ipsius obitu verisimiliter praesumatur." [10] It was held by some canonists that, although moral certitude is required of the death of a spouse whenever a second marriage is to be contracted publicly, with the authority of the Church, a probability of death would suffice where the parties were to be married privately *(auctoritate propria),* marriages of this kind being permitted before the Council of Trent.[11] However, this view was never accepted by the great majority of canonists.[12]

Another question which agitated canonists was whether one witness would suffice to prove the death of a spouse. Hostiensis held the affirmative of this proposition.[13] Abbas Antiquus also held this opinion.[14] Those who held this opinion took the phrase "certum nuncium" in the decretal of Clement III as being the accusative of "certus nuncius", masculine gender, and from this deduced that the Pope required one witness only for proof of death. The opposite opinion is well expressed by Sanchez, who would permit proof by one witness only in the case where a person died in a distant land and other proofs were not available. In such a contingency Sanchez required special qualities of trustworthiness in the one witness available.[15] The authors holding this latter opinion claimed that "certum nuncium" was the accusative of "certum nuncium", neuter gender; and that even if it were "certus nuncius", a person could not be considered "certus

[10] Hostiensis, in c. 5, X, *ut lite non contestata non procedatur ad testium receptionem vel ad sententiam diffinitivam,* II, 6; *Summa Aurea,* lib. IV, *de sponsa duorum,* n. 6.

[11] E.g., Pirhing, lib. IV, tit. I, § 5, n. 2.

[12] Cf. Sanchez, *De Sancto Matrimonii Sacramento,* lib. II, disp. 46, nn. 6, 9; Schmalzgrueber, lib. IV, tit. 21, n. 8.

[13] *Summa Aurea,* lib. IV, *de sponsa duorum,* n. 6.

[14] Glossa to c. 19, X, *de sponsalibus et matrimoniis,* IV, 1.

[15] *De Sancto Matrimonii Sacramento,* lib. II, disp. 46, nn. 11-12.

nuncius" if the only proof of death was his unsupported testimony.[16]

The third important question disputed by the authors was whether common opinion *(fama)* could be used to prove death. Panormitanus, representing the very strict viewpoint, denied that it would ever suffice.[17] Some authors claimed that this type of evidence in itself would suffice.[18] However, the best opinion of canonists was that common opinion would suffice only if it were bolstered by strong adminicular testimony.[19] Sanchez went into great detail in explaining how this kind of testimony should be gathered, and how it should be evaluated. The procedure outlined by him was largely followed by the instructions of the Holy See in the nineteenth century.[20]

An important point developed by the Decretalists, and well expressed by Sanchez, was that since it is not possible to prescribe everything that should enter into the establishing of certainty regarding the death of a spouse, it should be left to the discretion of a prudent judge who will take into account the various circumstances surrounding the case.[21] Statements similar to this are found in two important instructions of the Holy Office in the nineteenth century.[22]

16 Sanchez, *op. cit.*, lib. II, disp. 46, n. 11; Schmalzgrueber, lib. IV, tit. 21, n. 16; Reiffenstuel, lib. IV, tit. 21, n. 16.

17 In c. 19, X, *de sponsalibus et matrimoniis*, IV, 1.

18 Sanchez quotes several, *op. cit.*, lib. II, disp. 46, n. 14; Gonzales-Tellez (in c. 19, X, *de sponsalibus et matrimoniis*, IV, 1) quotes Xamar. as saying that *fama* with a lapse of five years would suffice to prove the death of an absent spouse.

19 Mascardus, *De Probationibus* (Venetiis, 1593), concl. 1074; Navarrus, *Opera Omnia* (Venetiis, 1618), tom. I, c. 22, n. 53; Sanchez, *De Sancto Matrimonii Sacramento*, lib. II, disp. 46, n. 15.

20 *Op. cit.*, lib. II, disp. 46, n. 16.

21 "Hinc fit cum certitudo mortis prioris viri, non omnino qualis debeat, praescribi possit, iudicis prudentis arbitrio attentis circumstantiis occurrentibus relinqui."—Sanchez, *De Sancto Matrimonii Sacramento*, lib. II, disp. 46, n. 7.

22 S.C.S. Off., instr. 12 iun. 1822—*Collectio Lacensis*, III, 557; S.C.S. Off., instr. 13 maii 1868, n. 5—*Fontes*, n. 1002.

C. *A Pre-Tridentine Council*

The provincial Council of Trier in 1310 decreed that anyone who against the prohibition of the Church contracted another marriage before obtaining certitude of the death of an absent spouse was to be haled before the bishop.[23]

D. *The Council of Trent*

The Council of Trent by outlawing clandestine marriages did much to simplify matters with regard to the proof of death of a husband or wife. Before the Council of Trent individuals could avoid the supervision of the Church by marrying privately when the first spouse had disappeared.[24] Navarrus (d. 1586) states that before the Council of Trent it frequently happened after a person had been married for a number of years and perhaps had raised a family, that the existence of a previous secret marriage would come to light; very often all trace of the first spouse was entirely lost.[25] The Council of Trent also declared that feigned absence did not dissolve the bond of marriage.[26]

E. *Councils and Synods*

The Council of Tours (1583) is very strict with regard to the proof of a spouse's death. It requires *testimonia certissima et indubitata* of the death of an absent spouse together with the permission of the bishop before another marriage.[27] Also strict is the wording of a decree of the Council of Cambrai (1631),

[23] Canon 93, n. 39: "Illi mittendi sunt ad dominum episcopum . . . mulier cuius vir diu abfuit et de illius morte certitudo non habetur, contra prohibitionem ecclesiae matrimonium cum alio contrahens, idem et de converso."—Mansi, XXV, 273.

[24] Kaas, *Kriegsverschollenheit und Wiederverheiratung* (Paderborn: Ferdinand Schöningh, 1919), p. 53.

[25] ". . . quod pro dolor frequenter contingebat ante Conc. Trid. . . . "—Navarrus, *Opera Omnia,* tom. I, c. 22, n. 53.

[26] "Canon 5. Si quis dixerit, propter haeresim, aut moestam cohabitationem, aut affectatam absentiam a coniuge dissolvi posse matrimonii vinculum: anathema sit."—Conc. Trid., sess. XXIV, *de matrimonio*—Denzinger-Bannwart, *Enchiridion,* n. 975.

[27] C. 9—Mansi, XXXIV A, 822.

which states that in cases of long absence death is not to be presumed, but must be proved, and no one may proceed to a second marriage until the death of the first spouse has been legitimately proved.[28] The third provincial Council of Mexico (1585), mindful of frauds which had been perpetrated, prescribed that no one already married should dare to contract another marriage because of the absence of the other spouse, unless the death of the first spouse was proved in accordance with law.[29]

It would seem that there were grave abuses with regard to the proof of death of an absent spouse in Northern Europe during the sixteenth and seventeenth centuries. This is to be deduced from the fact that so many diocesan synods of the period have legislation on the matter. The Synod of Besançon, France, of the year 1707, has a statute, taken from a previous synod held in the year 1604, which sheds light on the laxity in this regard which was to be found at this time. It states that the provisions of civil law have led many to the erroneous belief that a person is allowed to remarry after waiting for an absent spouse for a term of years. The Synod indicates the prevalence of this belief by calling it a common error. To stamp out this abuse the Synod forbade the priests of the diocese, under pain of excommunication, from allowing anyone, no matter how many years had elapsed, to contract another marriage, until it had been proved with certainty that the first spouse had died.[30]

A statute of the Synod of Malines, Belgium, 1609, widely quoted by other synods and also by the already mentioned Council of Cambrai (1631), after stating that certitude of death is necessary before a person can contract another marriage, insists that an absence of seven years, as many believe, or any other

[28] Tit. XIII, c. 14—Mansi, XXXVI (ter), 181.

[29] Lib. IV, tit. 1, § 11—*Concilium Mexicanum Provinciale III* (Mexico: typis mandatum cura, et expensis D.D. Francisci Antonii A Lorenzana, 1770), p. 82.

[30] Tit. XVII, n. 24—Hartzheim, *Concilia Germaniae* (Coloniae Augustae Agrippinensium, 1759-1790), X, 334.

term of years, does not suffice to permit another marriage.[31] A very odd statute is to be found in the Synod of Osnabrück, Germany, 1628, which requires that whenever one of the spouses is absent, and his death is not certain, the other must wait for at least seven years, and may not proceed to another marriage unless the case has been presented to the bishop or his *officialis,* and permission in writing for a new marriage has been obtained.[32]

The strict terminology of all these statutes is very noteworthy. There seems to be no provision for presumption of death in any cases.[33]

F. *Provincial Councils of the Eighteenth and Nineteenth Centuries*

The prevalence of a lax attitude among the Greek-Ruthenians (Oriental rite in union with Rome) towards the proof of death of an absent spouse may be ascertained from a decree of the

[31] "Cum ex longa coniugis absentia non resultet certitudo de eius obitu, et mors non praesumatur, sed probanda sit (quilibet enim vivere praesumitur), ad secundas nuptias convolare desiderans, Matrimonio non iungatur, nisi habita prius legitima certitudine de morte prioris coniugis; etiam si non septem tantum, ut multis persuasum est, sed etiam viginti; triginta et plures annos continuos eum abfuisse constiterit." Tit. IX, c. 10—Hartzheim, IX, 8. The same statute is also found in the following synods: Bois-le-Duc, Holland (1612), tit. X, c. 22—Hartzheim, IX, 220; Ghent, Belgium (1613), tit. IX, c. 9—Hartzheim, IX, 249; Ghent, Belgium, 1650, tit. IX, c. 10—Hartzheim, IX, 711; a very similar statute is found in the Synod of Cologne (1651), pars IV, c. 27—Hartzheim, IX, 776. The same legislation is expressed in a pastoral instruction of the Bishop of Ypres, Belgium (1768), c. 138—Hartzheim, X, 654.

[32] Pars I, c. 20, n. 11—Hartzheim, IX, 459. The same statute is found in the Synod of Paderborn, Germany (1688), tit. X, c. 17—Hartzheim, X, 165. This statute is very similar to the one contained in an earlier synod, that of Coutances, France (1609), tit. XVI, c. 29—Hartzheim, VIII, 874.

[33] Other synods which had legislation of a similar nature were Ypres, Belgium (1577), tit. XIX, c. 3—Hartzheim, VII, 856; Chur, Switzerland (1605), De Sacramento Matrimonii—Hartzheim, VIII, 650; Namur, Belgium (1639), tit. XIII, c. 9—Hartzheim, IX, 585; Strasbourg, France (1687), De Matrimonio—Hartzheim, X, 183; Chelmo, Poland (1745), c. 25—Hartzheim, X, 544.

provincial Council held at Zamość, Poland, in 1720. The decree mentions that even some of the pastors shared the common opinion that, when one of the parties was absent for more than seven years, the other was free to marry. The Council warned the pastors not to assist at the marriage of any such individuals, until the death of the absent party was proved to the satisfaction of the ordinary and his permission to contract another marriage was obtained. Any pastor who disobeyed this order was to be removed from his benefice, and otherwise punished according to the judgment of the bishop.[34]

The same abuse would seem to have been prevalent among the Maronites of this period, for a similar statute is to be found in the decrees of the provincial Council of Mount Lebanon, held in 1736.[35]

The bishops of Austria at a meeting held in Vienna in 1856 prepared an instruction for ecclesiastical judges in marriage cases, usually referred to as the *Instructio Austriaca.* This instruction drawn up by Cardinal Rauscher, the Archbishop of Vienna, and approved by Rome *in forma ordinaria,* had the force of law for all Austria, and was a strong directive force for foreign curiae. In cases where sufficient evidence was not forthcoming to arrive at moral certainty of the death of an absent spouse, the judges were advised to consult the civil

[34] "Parochus non audeat ad matrimonium recipere illos, quos constat aliquando vel uxorem vel maritum habuisse, nisi certo probetur illorum mors vel per testes vel alias legitimas probationes ab Ordinariis recipiendas, ac praevia ipsorum Ordinariorum licentia ac testimonio. Si secus fuerit, amoveatur a beneficio ac alias arbitrio Episcopi puniatur. Errorem illum inter rudiores etiam parochos fere communem, quod post discessum unius coniugis et per totum septennium non comparentis liberum sit alteri nubere, caveant, detestentur." Tit. III, § 8—*Collectio Lacensis,* II, 44.

[35] The wording of the two decrees is practically identical except that the Council of Mount Lebanon added: "Non enim sufficit prolixum huiusmodi tempus ad probandam alterius coniugis mortem, sed requiritur certitudo saltem moralis ex certis nuntiis hausta." Pars II, c. 11, § 25—*Collectio Lacensis,* II, 176. The same question is likewise treated by this council in a similar fashion in pars II, c. 11, § 10—*Collectio Lacensis,* II, 166.

authorities "cui ampliora suppetunt factum explorandi media et cuius est, mortis declarationem quoad effectus civiles edere." [36] The *Instructio Austriaca* required that cases of this kind should be tried by judicial procedure, with the *defensor vinculi* participating.[37]

As a result of the Civil War (1861-1865) in the United States doubts arose in many cases as to whether soldiers of whom no word had been received had been killed in battle. The Second Plenary Council of Baltimore, 1866, for this reason stressed the provisions of canon law on the question, and required that certain knowledge of the death of these missing persons had to be obtained before their wives could proceed to remarry, and that such questions should be settled by the Ordinary.[38]

Article II. The Sacred Congregations

The first important decree to emanate from the Sacred Congregations with reference to the proof of a spouse's death was an instruction from the Holy Office, *"Cum alias,"* of August 21, 1670. This instruction was sent out to warn bishops and pastors to use diligence in seeing that parties contemplating marriage were sufficiently questioned as to their freedom to

[36] Nn. 246-250—*Collectio Lacensis,* V, 1314-1315.

[37] N. 246—*Collectio Lacensis,* V, 1314.

[38] "Cum vero fieri possit, post luctuosas belli civilis vicissitudines, ut saepius dubia oriantur de morte coniugis, praesertim si militiae nomen dederit, opportunum ducimus hic Instructionis partem inserere quae a Congregatione S. Officii est edita a Rom. Pont. Clemente X probata (Aug. 21, 1670) et deinde omnibus Episcopis transmissa (25 Dec. 1827) : 'Interrogetur de loco . . . et sufficientes.' Qua in re prae oculis habendum illud Juris Canonici praescriptum ('In Praesentia.' 'Dominus ac Redemptor') iuxta quod mulieribus conjugatis non licet novum Matrimonium contrahere 'donec certum nuntium recipiant de morte virorum . . . quantocunque annorum numero ita remanere' debeant. Constat itaque, antequam novae nuptiae licite iniri possint, requiri certam prioris conjugis mortis cognitionem, quae nonisi ab Ordinario, omnibus bene perpensis, probari jure debet."—*Concilii Plenarii Baltimorensis II, Acta de Decreta* (Baltimore, 1868), n. 328. The decree of the Holy Office *"Ingentes bellorum clades"* of 1822 is to be found in Appendix 12 of the Council.

marry. Earlier instructions (these are not available) of the Holy Office on the same subject in 1658 and 1665 are mentioned. With regard to the proof of death of a spouse the instruction required a certificate of death from the hospital where the person died, or the church in which he was buried, or, in case of soldiers, from the commander of the regiment in which they had served. However, if these certificates were not obtainable, the Sacred Congregation stated that it did not intend to exclude other proofs, provided that they were legitimate and sufficient.[39]

About this time a serious problem had arisen in Transylvania. Many married people in this district had been taken prisoner by the enemy, and their spouses, not hearing from them, had contracted second marriages. It was the opinion of the clergy of the district that in such cases it was better to permit second marriages than to have the people be married by heretical ministers and thus lost to the Church. Therefore the clergy had been permitting this practice, on the condition that if the captives returned, the first unions should be restored. The Vicar Apostolic of the district wrote to the Holy See for a solution of the problem. Although he had been doing his best to prevent such invalid marriages, he gave it as his opinion that it was better to tolerate these marriages than to encourage the spread of heresy. The Holy Office, June 23, 1671, answered that these marriages could not be tolerated, that the clergy were to do everything in their power to discourage such invalid unions, and to separate the parties where the marriage had already taken place. The Holy Office told them to be governed by the decrees of Clement III and Lucius III on the matter, because there was no power in the world which could dispense in case of polygamy and adultery.[40]

An important case of proof of death was brought before the Congregation of the Council in 1733 and 1734. At the first

[39] S.C.S. Off., instr. 21 aug. 1670, n. 11—*Fontes,* n. 742. This instruction was reissued, 25 Dec. 1827, according to the Second Plenary Council of Baltimore, n. 328.

[40] S.C.S. Off., 23 iun. 1671—*Fontes,* n. 745.

hearing the main point at issue was the authenticity of a certificate of death for a soldier drawn up by the chaplain of the regiment; at the second hearing one witness was produced to prove the death of the soldier. After referring to the teaching of Sanchez, Gonzales-Tellez and Schmalzgrueber on the question, and quoting other cases in the past, the Congregation left the final decision to the judgment of the Bishop.[41]

Pius VI, in a letter to the Archbishop of Prague, July 11, 1789, touched on the question of proof of death of an absent spouse. He stated that long absence without news does not give rise to moral certitude of death.[42]

It is not until the latter part of the eighteenth century that the Holy See permitted marriage where there was only a presumption of the death of one of the spouses. In the early eighteenth century the very least which the Holy Office would accept as sufficient for proof of death was the testimony of one trustworthy eye-witness.[43]

There are two documents emanating from the Holy See in the late eighteenth century in which remarriage after presump-

[41] S.C.C., *in Papiensi. Matrimonii,* 12 dec. 1733 et 27 febr. 1734—*Thesaurus Resolutionum S.C.C.,* VI (1733-1734), 181, 215. The Congregation of the Council decided another very important case in 1860, in which the whole question of the proof of a spouse's death was thoroughly discussed.—S.C.C., *in Mediolan. Matrimonii,* 22 sept. 1860—Pallottini, "Matrimonium", § 14, nn. 36-41, 56-64.

[42] Kutschker, *Das Eherect der katholischen Kirche* (Wien, 1856), I, 218. Reference is made to this letter in the instruction of the Holy Office in 1868.—*Fontes,* n. 1002.

[43] Giraldi, in a work first published in 1719 (*Expositio Iuris Pontificii,* Romae, 130, II, Sectio 656), says: "Sed cum Doctores discrepent in statuendo qualis debeat esse certitudo de morte prioris coniugis, antequam alter superstes transeat ad secunda vota, relictis privatis eorundem Doctorum opinionibus, crederem, habendam esse pro certa regula praxim Tribunalis S. Inquisitionis, a quo huiusmodi transitus nunquam permittitur, nisi constet de morte coniugis vel per authenticum testimonium seu fidem, puta praefecti nosocomii, aut alterius loci, in quo forte decesserit, sive Rectoris Ecclesiae, in qua sepultus fuerit, sive etiam per iuratum testimonium duorum testium, deponentium de visu obitus, aut etiam unius tantum, omni exceptione maioris."

tion of the death of one of the spouses is permitted. In an instruction of unknown date sent to an Austrian bishop at the instance of Pius VI (1775-1799) presumption of the death of a spouse was permitted, provided that it gave rise to moral certitude. [44] The Sacred Congregation for the Propagation of the Faith issued an important instruction in 1792 on the proof of death in cases of disappearance. Even when there were no witnesses of the person's death, remarriage was permitted to the other spouse if there were conjectures of the individual's death sufficiently strong to induce moral certitude.[45] This instruction also stated that when people had remarried in good faith, believing that the loss of their spouses in times of war, famine and like calamities, justified this course of action, they were to be left in good faith, "quia bonae fidei possessor turbari a possessione non debet."

The Holy Office issued another instruction on the proof of a spouse's death in 1822. For the most part this instruction followed that of 1670. However, it devoted attention to the case where it is impossible to get direct testimony concerning the death of a husband or wife. The instruction stated that even if the various proofs offered did not suffice, if taken separately, to prove death, they may produce certainty when taken together. For this reason there is a place for presumptions and conjectures, which serve to confirm the testimony of witnesses. Common opinion, proven facts which suppose death,

[44] "Si a muliere aut viro petatur transitus ad alias nuptias ob praesumtam mortem coniugum, a longo tempore absentium, magno poterit esse adiumento resolutio, quam Sanctus Dominus Noster sequentem in modum efformavit: ad probandam mortem alterius ex coniugibus sufficere veram moralem certitudinem, etiam sine teste de visu."—Kutschker, *Das Eherect,* I, 233.

[45] " . . . aut tales coniecturae de illius interitu intervenire debent, quae prudentem virum ita plane esse morali quadam certitudine persuadeant." S.C. de Prop. Fide, instr. a. 1792—*Fontes,* n. 4632. This instruction was referred to as a guide in establishing proof of a spouse's death in a response of the Holy Office in 1851—S.C.S. Off., 12 febr. 1851—*Fontes,* n. 915.

and hearsay evidence can be used in this connection.[46] This instruction was reissued at various times, e.g., June 28, 1865 and Nov. 21, 1866.[47] It was superseded by the fuller instruction of 1868. The presumption of death of a spouse is mentioned again in a reply of the Holy Office in 1865.[48]

The Holy Office in 1868 issued a very complete instruction on the proof of death of a husband or wife, which is still the norm used in settling problems of this kind, as is evident from recent decrees of the Holy See. This instruction may be briefly summarized thus:

(1) Long absence in itself is no proof of death.

(2) An authentic document proving death is to be obtained if possible.

(3) If a document of this kind is not available, the testimony of two trustworthy eye-witnesses will suffice.

(4) The Holy Office will accept the testimony of one eye-witness, provided that he is trustworthy and his testimony is confirmed by adminicular evidence; if the latter is lacking, the

[46] "Verum in tantis, quibus saepe huiusmodi mortis probationes premuntur difficultatibus, S.C. nullam respuit, quae aliquid ad fidem faciendam valeat, ut perspicere possit, an pluribus quandoque concurrentibus, quae seorsim certitudinem sufficientem parere nequeunt, omnia tamen simul iuncta hanc efficiant. Hinc datur locus praesumptionibus et coniecturis, quibus testium dicta confirmentur, publicae vocis, et famae ratio habetur, certa facta authentica probata, quae mortem supponant, expenruntur. Etiam contigit, ut testium fide dignorum probe informatorum dicta tempore non suspecto ab aliis percepta fuerint; testes autem immediati vel morte vel absentia, aut alia de causa audiri nequeant, habeantur vero dicta testium de alieno dicto deponentium: qui tamen omnibus pensatis prudenti mortis secutae iudicio satis esse censeantur." S. C. S. Off., instr. 12 iun. 1822—*Concilii Plenarii Baltimorensis II, Acta et Decreta,* Appendix 12, p. 308; *Collectio Lacensis,* III, 557; *AKKR,* XXII (1869), 186.

[47] S. C. S. Off., 28 iun. 1865—*Fontes,* n. 984; S. C. S. Off., 21 nov. 1866—*Fontes,* n. 997.

[48] " . . . nisi forte ex pluribus saltem coniecturis (quae sin minus singulae, at certe simul coniunctae certitudinem moralem pariant) demonstrari possit legitimum eorum coniugem mortem vere obiise." S. C. S. Off., 31 maii 1865, ad 3, 4, 7—*Fontes,* n. 983.

testimony of one eye-witness will be acceptable provided that there is nothing inconsistent or improbable in his testimony.

(5) If no other evidence is available, hearsay evidence will be acceptable if it is in conformity with the circumstances of the case, and is such as to induce a prudent judgment of death.

(6) If no witnesses of any kind may be obtained, the proof of death may be made from conjectures, presumptions, clues, and various circumstances, but these must be of such a nature and so confirm one another, that they lead to moral certitude of the death of the person in question. The Holy Office gives specific directions as to how evidence of this nature is to be obtained, and how it should be weighed.

(7) If after judging a case according to these rules laid down by the Holy Office, the question is still uncertain, the matter should be referred to the Holy See.[49]

Another instruction of importance in this question is the instruction of the Congregation of the Propagation of the Faith of the year 1883. This instruction follows the rules as laid down in the instruction of 1868. It lays special stress on proof of death when no witnesses are available and when in consequence of this lack of witnesses the proof or moral certitude of death hinges upon the various factors connected with the question of presumption of death. Minute and careful instructions are given in this regard.[50] In reply to a request for an authentic interpretation of a section of the instruction of 1883, the Holy Office in 1891 replied by quoting the instruction of 1868.[51] With regard to soldiers who, in the Italian campaign to annex Abyssinia to Eritrea, disappeared after the battle of Adua (or Adowa), on March 1, 1896, and regarding whom there was proof that they were certainly in the battle, the Holy Office in 1898 permitted their former wives to remarry.[52] After the earthquake of Messina and Reggio of Dec. 28, 1908, in which

[49] S. C. S. Off., instr. 13 maii 1868—*Fontes,* n. 1002. The complete text of this instruction will be found in the Appendix to this study, p. 133.

[50] S. C. de Prop. Fide, instr. a. 1883, nn. 41-43—*Fontes,* n. 4901.

[51] S. C. S. Off., 8 maii 1891—*Fontes,* n. 1135.

[52] S. C. S. Off., 20 iul. 1898—*ASS,* XXXI (1898-1899), 252.

many persons disappeared, the Congregation of the Sacraments in 1910 stated that the particular cases arising out of the disaster should be settled by the instruction of 1868.[53] The more recent decrees of the Congregation have invariably settled cases involving proof of a spouse's death according to the instruction of 1868.[54]

The number of decrees which have been issued from the Sacred Congregations since the sixteenth century on the proof of death of a spouse is quite large; only the most significant have been mentioned in this chapter.[55]

Summary of Historical Synopsis

Roman Law is of great importance in this question as its

[53] S. C. de Sacr., 12 mart. 1910—*AAS*, II (1910), 196.

[54] S. C. de Sacr., 28 nov., 18 dec. 1914—*Fontes,* n. 2109; S. C. de Sacr., 29 apr. 1915—*Fontes,* n. 2111; S. C. de Sacr., 25 iun. 1915—*Fontes,* n. 2112; S. C. de Sacr., 25 febr. 1916—*Fontes,* n. 2115; S. C. de Sacr., 19 ian. 1917—*Fontes,* n. 2117; S. C. de Sacr., 18 nov. 1920—*AAS,* XIV (1922), 96.

[55] Among the other decrees from the Sacred Congregations concerning proof of death the following may be mentioned: S. C. C. *in Aversana,* apr. 1587—Pallottini, "Matrimonium," § 14, n. 68; S. C. C., *in Venetiarum,* 15 nov. 1604—Pallottini, "Matrimonium," § 14, n. 45; S. C. Ep. et Reg., 24 nov. 1662—*Fontes,* n. 1799; S. C. C., *in Bovinen. Matrimonii,* 28 sept. 1697—Pallottini, "Matrimonium," § 14, nn. 50-51; S. C. C., *in Avenionem Matrimonii,* 5 apr. 1704, 4 dec. 1706, 12 ian. 1708, 8 feb. 1710—Pallottini, "Matrimonium," § 14, n. 52: S. C. C., *in Smirnen. Matrimonii,* 6 maii et 9 sept. 1752—*Thesaurus Resolutionum S. C. C.*, XVI (1752), 66, 119; S. C. de Prop. Fide, 21 apr. 1788—*Fontes,* n. 4620; S. C. C., 22 aug. 1840—*Fontes,* n. 4070; S. C. S. Off., 24 febr. 1847—*Collectanea S. C. de Prop. Fide,* (2. ed.), n. 1011, I, 549; S. C. S. Off., 22 mart. 1865—*Fontes,* n. 982; S. C. S. Off., 28 iun. 1865—*Fontes,* n. 984; S. C. S. Off., 21 nov. 1866—*Fontes,* n. 997; S. C. S. Off., 13 sept. 1871—*AKKR,* XXVII (1872), 111; S. C. S. Off., 2 apr. 1873—*Collectanea,* 2. ed., n. 1399; S. C. S. Off., 27 (or 17) apr. 1887—Gasparri, *Tractatus Canonicus de Matrimonio,* n. 563, also found in *AER,* VIII (1893), 144; S. C. C., 14 dec. 1889—*ASS,* XXII (1889-1890), 546; S. C. S. Off., instr. (ad Ep. Orient.), 22 aug. 1890—*Fontes,* n. 1128; S. C. S. Off., 18 iul. 1900—*AKKR,* LXXXI (1901), 345, also found in *AER,* XXIV (1901), 387; S. C. de Sacr., 16 dec. 1910—*Fontes,* n. 2104; S. R. R., 19 oct. 1928, dec. XLIX—*Decisiones,* XX (1928), 426; S. R. R., 27 iul. 1929, dec. XL—*Decisiones,* XXI (1929), 339.

provisions governing the proof of death in marriage cases conflicted in certain points with the law of the Church, and since throughout the centuries the civil authorities continued to make use of Justinian's provisions in settling the various difficulties that arose in the matter. Justinian decreed that in cases of long absence a person could not contract another marriage unless the death of the first spouse was proved by documentary evidence; he made an exception in cases of captivity, when a person could proceed to a new marriage after five years, if it was uncertain whether the captured spouse was alive or dead.

In the early Eastern Church a person was forbidden to contract a new marriage unless certitude had been obtained of the death of the first spouse.

The fifth century decretals of Pope Innocent I and Pope St. Leo I required that, when individuals had been taken prisoner, and their wives had remarried, the first unions had to be restoreα if the captives obtained there freedom. These two letters determined the attitude of the Church in the question of long absence.

Many of the penitentials were lax, permitting remarriage after a term of years in such cases. The eighth century Councils ot Verberies and Compiègne had equally lax provisions.

The decretals of Gregory IX contained letters of Lucius Ill and Clement III requiring certitude of the death of one's spouse before a person could proceed to another marriage.

The decretalists disputed on three points: (1) whether moral certitude or only moral probability was necessary before a person could proceed to another marriage; (2) whether one witness would suffice to prove death; and (3) whether common opinion (*fama*) would be enough to prove the death of an absent spouse.

The Council of Trent, by outlawing clandestine marriages, furnished the Church a better opportunity to enforce the provisions of canon law with regard to the proof of a spouse's death. A number of subsequent councils and synods had legislation on the matter to correct abuses which had arisen in certain section.

From the sixteenth century onward there is a large number

of decrees of the Sacred Congregations on the proof of a spouse's death. All insist on moral certitude of the death of an absent spouse before a person may proceed to another marriage. The decrees and instructions of the Holy Office in the nineteenth century permit presumption of death in such cases, provided that it is sufficiently strong to give moral certitude of the death of the absent person. The most important of these documents is the instruction of the Holy Office of the year of 1868, which is the norm used at present by the Sacred Congregations in settling difficulties that arise in connection with the proof of a spouse's death.

PART TWO

CANONICAL COMMENTARY

Chapter IV

GENERAL FEATURES OF PROCEDURE IN ESTABLISHING PROOF OF DEATH

Article I. Instruction of the Year 1868

The process for proving the death of a husband or wife, so as to establish freedom to contract a second marriage, is not directly mentioned in the Code.[1] However the question is covered in the Code by can. 1069, § 2:

> Quamvis prius matrimonium sit irritum aut solutum qualibet ex causa, non ideo licet aliud contrahere, antequam de prioris nullitate aut solutione legitime et certo constiterit.

By requiring certainty of the solution of a first marriage before a person may proceed to the second, the Code has retained the same general rule which was laid down in the old canon law.[2]

Before the Code the instruction of the year 1868 was the norm followed in cases of this kind.,[3] and there can be no doubt that it is still applicable in such cases.

That the instruction of 1868 is still to be followed in questions involving the proof of death of a former spouse is evident from a post-Code decision of the Congregation of the Sacraments. Before handing down a decision in the case, the Congregation requested the Ordinary to complete the investigations according to the instruction of 1868, and if unable then to come to a

[1] It is mentioned indirectly in canon 1053.

[2] C. 2, X, *de secundis nuptiis,* IV, 21; c. 19; X, *de sponsalibus et matrimoniis,* IV, 1.

[3] " . . . Instructio S. C. S. Off., an. 1868, a qua tota haec regitur quaestio. . . . Expendendos esse ab Ordinario casus particulares iuxta Instructionem 'Matrimonii Vinculo,' a S. C. Sancti Officii, datam anno 1868." S. C. de Sacr., 12 mart. 1910—*AAS,* II (1910), 196. Cf. also: S. C. S. Off., 8 maii 1891, ad I et II—*Fontes,* n. 1135; S. C. de Sacr., 29 apr. 1915—*Fontes,* n. 2111; S. C. de Sacr., 25 iun. 1915—*Fontes,* n. 2112; S. C. de Sacr., 25 febr. 1916—*Fontes,* n. 2115.

decision to send the *acta* of the case to the Congregation.[4] In the two Rota decisions published since the Code which touched on this question the instruction of 1868 was quoted as authoritative in the matter.[5] The authors are in agreement that the instruction of 1868 is to be used in cases of proof of death of a former spouse.[6]

The instruction of 1868 consists of a lengthy preamble and eleven paragraphs. In the preamble the reasons which led the Holy Office to issue the instruction are set forth. The increased facilities for travel together with the constant stream of emigration from Europe to other parts of the world had given rise to a great number of cases involving the proof of death of a husband or wife. As a result the Holy See had been overwhelmed with cases of this kind. The instruction was issued to acquaint the Ordinaries with the practice of the Holy Office in settling cases of proof of death, so that they might be able to settle as many cases as possible without recourse to the Holy See, and so that where recourse to the Holy See was found necessary, the case would be so written as to make an early decision possible.[7]

[4] S.C. de Sacr., 18 nov. 1920—*AAS,* XIV (1922), 96. The Sacred Congregation of the Sacraments in an instruction issued to the Italian bishops in connection with the provisions, relative to the civil effects of marriage, of the Concordat of 1929 with the Italian government, directed the bishops to use the instruction of 1868 in cases of presumed death arising out of the World War.—S.C. de Sacr., 1 iul. 1929, n. 48—*AAS,* XXI (1929), 360.

[5] S.R.R., 19 oct. 1928, dec. XLIX—*Decisiones,* XX (1928), 426; S.R.R., 27 iul. 1929, dec. XL—*Decisiones,* XXI (1929), 339.

[6] Gasparri, *De Matrimonio* (ed. nova), I, n. 562; Cappello, *De Matrimonio,* n. 393; Triebs, *Praktisches Handbuch des geltenden kanonischen Eherechts* (Breslau: Ostdeutsche Verlaganstalt, 1933), p. 311; Schaaf, "Proof of Death of Husband or Wife"—*AER,* LXXXIX (1933), 285.

[7] "Quapropter Sacra eadem Congregatio . . . e re esse censuit, uberiorem edere Instructionem in qua . . . regulae indigitentur, quas in eiusmodi casibus haec ipsa S. Congr. sequi solet, ut illarum ope, vel absque necessitate recursus ad Sanctam Sedem, possint iudicia ferri: vel certe, si recurrendum sit, status questionis ita dilucide exponatur, ut impediri longiori mora sententia non debeat." S.C.S. Off., 13 maii 1868—*Fontes,* n. 1002.

Two main ideas permeate the instruction; one that the unity of marriage must be protected at all costs, especially against fraud and deception; the other that everything possible must be done to give a person the opportunity to exercise the freedom of remarriage after the death of his first spouse. The Holy See did not wish to see people forced to remain celibate after the death of their first spouse, and for this reason was desirous of having cases of doubtful death settled as quickly as possible.

Article II. Administrative Procedure

When a case involving the proof of death of an absent husband or wife in order to permit the surviving spouse to remarry comes before the Ordinary, it will as a rule be handled in an administrative process. Although there is apparently nothing to prevent the Ordinary from settling the question through a judicial process if he so desires, it may be said that this process is essentially an administrative one. In the first place it partakes of the nature of a *status liber* case which is primarily administrative.[8] This view is further strengthened by the fact that since 1908 such cases have been handled exclusively by the Sacred Congregation of the Sacraments, which is competent to handle administrative matters only.[9] Besides, the nature of the process, which involves the establishing of a fact, lends itself better to the administrative method.[10] In addition, the fact that this process is not mentioned among the judicial processes included in the first part of the Fourth Book of the Code indicates that it is essentially administrative, since the authors are agreed that the processes not mentioned in this particular section of the Code are administrative.[11]

[8] De Smet, *De Sponsalibus et Matrimonio* (4. ed., Brugis: Car. Beyaert, 1927), nn. 565, 702 c.

[9] In the two Rota decisions (S. R. R., 19 oct. 1928, dec. XLIX—*Decisiones,* XX (1928), 426; S. R. R., 27 iul. 1929, dec. XL—*Decisiones,* XXI (1929), 339) that have touched the question of proof of death ot a spouse, nullity causes were involved.

[10] S. C. C., 14 dec. 1889—*ASS,* XXII (1889-1890), 546.

[11] Maroto, *Institutiones Iuris Canonici* (Romae, 1919), I, n. 724; Coronata, *Institutiones Iuris Canonici* (Taurini: Marietti, 1933-1939), I, n. 282.

A. *Administrative Procedure in General*

Since almost all cases involving the proof of death of a former spouse will be settled by the Ordinary administratively, it is well to preface some remarks about the administrative process in general, and to note especially in what particulars it differs from the judicial process. Much light on the question of administrative procedure is cast by the canons from 2142-2194, which deal explicitly with certain administrative processes.

There are several other matrimonial proceedings that are rightly considered administrative and which are by nature not judicial. The process used in the pre-nuptial investigation of the freedom to marry is administrative by nature;[12] the procedure in declaring a marriage null due to lack of form is also administrative;[13] the process for dissolution of a *matrimonium ratum sed non consummatum* is administrative by nature, although minute details of judicial procedure are used;[14] whether the process of canon 1990 is administrative or judicial is still a matter of controversy.[15]

Before the Code, judicial procedure was divided into ordinary and summary procedure. For marriage causes which involved the

[12] Canons 1019-1034.

[13] Pontificia Commissio ad Codicis Canones Authentice Interpretandos, 16 oct. 1919—*AAS,* XI (1919), 479.

[14] S. C. de Sacr., 7 maii 1923—*AAS,* XV (1923), 392.

[15] Cf. Kay, *Competence in Matrimonial Procedure* (The Catholic University of America, Canon Law Studies, n. 53, Washington: The Catholic University of America, 1929), pp. 109-142; cf. also Kennedy, *The Special Matrimonial Process in Cases of Evident Nullity* (The Catholic University of America, Canon Law Studies, n. 93, Washington: The Catholic University of America, 1935), pp. 51-76. The former holds that the process of canon 1990 is judicial, the latter that it is administrative. However, in a recently published decision of the Rota (S. R. R., 20 iun. 1931, dec. XXIX—*Decisiones,* XXIII [1931], 252), it is stated that the process of canon 1990 is administrative, not judicial. The instruction of the Sacred Congregation of the Sacraments, issued on August 15, 1936 (*AAS,* XXVIII [1936], 313-361), likewise seems to indicate that the process of canon 1990 is administrative, by requiring, in article 228, that the *Officialis* must have a special mandate from the Ordinary to handle this process.

bond ordinary procedure was obligatory.[16] This distinction was abolished by the Code.[17] A good deal of the confusion to be found with regard to the question of proof of death of a former spouse is due to the failure to keep the foregoing fact in mind.

The term *summary* is often used, since the Code, to designate administrative processes. For example, the administrative processes of the third part of the Fourth Book are so designated in the Index to the Code. Moreover, canon 2145, § 1, states: "In his processibus summarie procedendum est." However, care must be taken not to confuse these processes with the pre-Code summary process which was a real judicial process. For this reason the term *administrative* process seems preferable. Although it is not used explicitly in the Code it is implicitly designated in canons 250-251 where the dstinction is made between processes "ordine iudicario" and processes "in linea disciplinari." The term, "administrative," is most commonly used by authors.[18]

A process is defined by Noval as a complexus or series of acts and solemnities, which are prescribed by law for the settlement of questions or the expediting of affairs by public authority.[19]

Before the Code, the difference between judicial and administrative processes was on the whole difficult to determine; this was due in no small measure to the fact that before 1908 the Sacred

[16] Benedictus XIV, const. *"Dei Miseratione,"* 3 nov. 1741—*Fontes,* n. 318. When judicial procedure was used (before the Code) with regard to the proof of death of a former spouse, the summary procedure was permitted, since in cases of this kind not the bond of marriage but the existence of the marriage itself was involved.—S. C. C., 14 dec. 1889—*ASS,* XXII (1889-1890), 546.

[17] Roberti, *De Processibus,* I, nn. 3, 5; Noval, *De Processibus* (Romae: Marietti, 1920), I, n. 35; Noval, *De Processibus* (2. ed., Romae: Marietti, 1932), II, n. 458 (In this work when volume I of Noval, *De Processibus,* is quoted, the first edition is indicated; when volume II is quoted, the second edition is indicated).

[18] Noval, *De Processibus,* II, nn. 458-459; Coronata, *Institutiones Iuris Canonici,* III, n. 1573.

[19] "Nomine *processus,* si is *subiective* sumatur, venit in iure *complexus* vel *series actuum et solemnitatum, quae a lege praescribuntur pro quaestionibus pertractandis aut negotiis expediendis publica auctoritate."*—Noval, I, n. 4.

Congregations handled judicial and administrative processes indiscriminately. The reform of the Roman Curia in 1908, by restoring the power and prestige of the Roman tribunals and limiting the Roman congregations for the most part to administrative matters, was a step on the road to clarification of the distinction between the two kinds of process, judicial and administrative.[20]

While it is not always possible to make a perfect distinction between judicial and administrative processes (the process of canon 1990 is a case in point), there can be no doubt that the Code, profiting from the systems in vogue in modern states, has made a profound if not too explicit distinction between administrative and judicial power, both with regard to the agencies which exercise it and the processes themselves.[21]

The Code has helped to clarify the question by making a clear cut distinction between voluntary and judicial jurisdiction. Jurisdiction is divided into voluntary or non-judicial and contentious or judicial.[22] The distinction between the two is based rather on the manner in which the jurisdiction is exercised, than on the objects with which they are concerned. Thus, voluntary or non-judicial jurisdiction is that which is exercised without a strictly judicial form, while contentious jurisdiction must be exercised in a strictly judicial form. Non-judicial jurisdiction is divided into legislative, administrative and favorable (*gratiosa*).[23]

The essential difference between a judicial and an administrative process is to be found in the legitimate form of these processes. This form is both intrinsic and extrinsic. With regard to the intrinsic form, the judical process supposes a conflict between two parties (*in contradictorio*), while in the administrative process there is but one party, even though several persons invoke the same act of the judge. Concerning the extrinsic form,

[20] Roberti, *De Processibus,* nn. 37, 81.

[21] Roberti, *De Processibus,* I, n. 37.

[22] Canon 201.

[23] Maroto, *Institutiones Iuris Canonici,* I, n. 734; Doheny, *Canonical Procedure in Marriage Cases* (Milwaukee: The Bruce Publishing Co., 1938), p. 142; Coronata, *Institutiones Iuris Canonici,* I, n. 282.

specified acts and solemnities are required and prescribed by the supreme authority so that a certain form of proceeding may be considered a judicial process.

In an administrative process judicial acts and solemnities are not required; in addition to the special prescriptions laid down by the legislator, only those acts and solemnities are needed which by virtue of the natural law and right reason are necessary for the proper investigation and just decision of the question proposed in a particular case.[24]

An administrative process, although it is not strictly a trial, imitates a trial to a certain extent. The many solemnities of a trial are not required, e.g., the presenting of the *libellus,* the *litis contestatio,* etc.; but whatever is required by the natural law for trials in general must be present, for example, the hearing of the parties, the determination of the controversy, proofs and defenses, the notification of the interested parties of the decision, and the possibility of recourse against the decision.[25] In addition, whatever specific prescriptions of the positive law have been made with regard to a particular administrative process must be carried out. For example, the various regulations laid down in canons 2142-2194 must be observed when the processes therein described are used; with regard to the proof of death of a former spouse the provisions of the instruction of the year 1868 will have to be carried out. Justice and natural equity will as a rule demand that all the acts of an administrative process be put in writing and authenticated.[26]

The Bishop as both a judge and an administrator can act either

[24] Noval, *De Processibus,* I, n. 23, II, n. 450; Roberti, *De Processibus,* I, nn. 37, 52. Noval (II, n. 450) seems to place the distinction between judicial and administrative processes more in the extrinsic than in the intrinsic form. Roberti (I, n. 52) on the other hand finds the main difference between the two processes in the intrinsic form.

[25] Coronata, *Institutiones Iuris Canonici,* III, n. 1573; Noval, *De Processibus,* I, n. 28, II, nn. 450, 462.

[26] Noval, *De Processibus,* II, n. 462. Coronata (*Institutiones Iuris Canonici,* III, n. 1123, nota 3) notes that from canon 1585 ("Cuilibet processui . . . ") it is clear that the presence of a notary is required in all processes, not merely in judicial processes.

in a judicial or in an administrative capacity. In administrative processes the Bishop acts in his capacity of administrator and not as a judge in his diocese; as administrator he exercises a power operating for a speedy settlement of problems for the good of souls, a power that ordinarily is not restrained by the fullness of judicial forms, although imitating them to obtain certainty.

Administrative processes may be handled by those who are listed as Ordinaries in canon 198. Included are not only the Roman Pontiff but also, within their respective territories, a residential bishop, an abbot and a prelate *nullius,* their vicars general, an administrator, a vicar apostolic and all those who by the provisions of law or by approved constitutions succeed during a vacancy to any of these offices; for their own subjects major superiors in clerical exempt religious institutes are Ordinaries.

It should be noted that in accordance with canon 381, § 1, the Vicar General is competent to take charge of an administrative process, except in those cases where the Bishop has reserved it to himself, or where by law a special mandate on the part of the bishop is required. The *officialis,* who has ordinary power in trials, is not competent in administrative processes unless he has been delegated by the bishop, for canon 1573 which treats of his appointment ascribes to him only judicial power.

The Ordinary in handling administrative processes has a certain latitude which is not allowed in judicial processes, but he must be careful to follow whatever prescriptions have been laid down by the positive law for the particular process at hand, and in all such processes he must proceed in accordance with the natural law, and endeavor to solve the question presented in accordance with justice and equity.

In an administrative procedure the competence of the Ordinary to accept the case will not be established by canons 1557-1568 or by canon 1964 which refer to judicial procedure, but by canon 201, §§ 1 and 3, which regulates administrative acts. By virtue of canon 201 the Ordinary is competent to preside at an administrative process whenever the person presenting the petition is his subject.

When the Ordinary issues a decree after an administrative process, no appeal as such is permitted, but recourse against the decree to the competent Sacred Congregation is permitted.[27] It should be noted that there is no provision in law for a recourse to the metropolitan against the decrees of an ordinary in an administrative matter,[28] and canon 1601 states that no appeal or recourse to the Sacred Rota is permitted against the decree of an Ordinary; the statement of the canon that the Sacred Congregations have exclusive competence in such recourses indicates that the incompetence of the Rota in such cases is absolute.[29] Furthermore, the Pontifical Commission for the Interpretation of the Code has decided that the Sacred Congregations have exclusive competence in actions against the decrees of Ordinaries pertaining to the administration of their dioceses.[30]

There is some difference in the terminology employed in judicial and administrative processes. The term *cause* (*causa*) is used when speaking of strictly judicial processes, *case* (*casus*) in connection with administrative processes. *Sentence* (*sententia*) and *appeal* (*appellatio*) are terms used with regard to judicial procedure, *decree* (*decretum*) and *recourse* (*recursus*) when it is a question of administrative procedure. The terms *accusation* (*accusatio*), *plaintiff* (*actor*) and *advocate* (*advocatus*) are used in connection with judicial procedure, while *petition* (*petitio*), *petitioner* (*orator*) and *counsellor* (*consultor*) are the corres-

[27] The term recourse was introduced by the Code. Before the promulgation of the Code, appeals were ordinarily classified as judicial or extra-judicial.—Connolly, *Appeals* (The Catholic University of America, Canon Law Studies, n. 79, Washington: The Catholic University of America, 1932), p. 4. An appeal was said to be extra-judicial when it was interposed against administrative decrees of a superior or a judge.—Bouix, *Tractatus de Iudiciis Ecclesiasticis* (Parisiis, 1855), II, 246.

[28] With regard to the administrative processes in the third part of the Fourth Book of the Code, canon 2146, § 1, states that the only remedy in law against a decree of the Ordinary in these processes is recourse to the Holy See. Cf. also canon 2194.

[29] Noval, *De Processibus,* I, n. 174.

[30] Pontificia Commissio ad Codicis Canones Authentice Interpretandos, 22 maii 1923—*AAS,* XVI (1924), 251.

ponding terms employed when administrative procedure is followed. *Definire* is a judicial term; *declarare* is used in both judicial and administrative procedure. The term *judge* (*iudex*) while more properly used in connection with judicial procedure, is also used with regard to administrative processes.

In this study the procedure for establishing the proof of death of a husband or wife will be treated as an administrative process. Wherever reference is made to the procedure as a judicial process, this will be expressly mentioned.

B. *Administrative Procedure in Proof of Death*

When the Ordinary decides to handle a case of proof of death of a spouse in administrative procedure, it is proper for him to keep in mind that he should be guided by the following practice:

(1) In handling the case the Ordinary should follow the prescriptions of the instruction of 1868. He should also make use of the other instructions and published decisions of the Holy See with regard to proof of death, as these will often lead to a better understanding of the provisions of the instruction of 1868.[31]

(2) The competence of the Ordinary for an administrative process with regard to the proof of death of a former spouse will be determined not by canon 1561 or canon 1964, but by canon 201,[32] which permits direct jurisdiction only over subjects. It would seem that this canon is broad enough to permit an Ordinary to handle administratively marriage cases of non-subjects, as long as an interested third party is his subject. since the canon acknowledges an indirect jurisdiction.[33]

(3) The *officialis* is not competent to undertake the administrative process for proof of death. To proceed in this matter, he needs the delegation of the Ordinary. The Vicar General, however, is competent, without delegation, since he is not excluded by law from handling this process.[34]

(4) The presence of the *defensor vinculi* is not necessary.[35]

[31] Cf. *supra*, pp. 30-36

[32] Cf. *supra*, p. 48.

[33] Maroto, *Institutiones Iuris Canonici*, I, n. 727.

[34] Cf. *supra*, p. 48.

[35] Cf. *supra*, p. 52.

(5) The petitioner should be permitted to have a counsellor. If the petitioner is poor the Ordinary should see that a counsellor is appointed for him. The extensive investigation required for this process calls for the presence of someone trained in canon law to assist the parties in gathering the necessary evidence.

(6) The acts should be in writing. This will require the presence of a notary in the conducting of the process. The necessity of having the acts in writing is due, among other reasons, to the fact that if the case is forwarded to Rome the acts or authentic copies thereof must be sent along with the recourse.[36]

(7) This process must not be confused with the documentary process of canon 1990 which is used in cases where the nullity of a marriage is claimed.

(8) After the manner of the Sacred Congregations the Ordinary should consult with canonists and theologians in arriving at his decision.[37]

Article III. Judicial Procedure

If the Ordinary so desires, he may use judicial procedure [38] to decide a case where a declaration of the death of a husband or wife is sought. If judicial procedure is used, the regulations laid down in the instruction of 1868 must be followed as in an administrative process.

Since the bond of marriage is not involved in the process for proof of the death of a spouse, but only the existence of the marriage itself, several special points must be kept in mind when judicial procedure is used:

(1) One judge will suffice, for a tribunal of three judges is required only in marriage causes affecting the bond.[39] However,

[36] S. C. C. Off., instr. 13 maii 1868, n. 11—*Fontes,* n. 1002.

[37] S. C. S. Off., instr. 13 maii 1868, n. 10.

[38] Kaas (*Kriegsverschollenheit und Wiederverheiratung,* p. 91) and Wernz-Vidal (*Ius Canonicum* [Romae: Apud Aedes Universitatis Gregorianae, 1925-1938], V, n. 255) erroneously suggest the use of the summary judicial process abolished by the Code.

[39] Canon 1576, § 1, n. 1.

the Ordinary can give the case to a tribunal of three judges if he deems it advisable.[40]

(2) The presence of the *defensor vinculi* is not necessary,[41] although he may take part in the case where it is required by local statute.[42] However, it would be proper for the Ordinary to require the presence of the promoter of justice in the interest of safeguarding the public good.[43]

(3) Furthermore, two concordant sentences are not necessary. The interested parties may appeal if they wish; if the *defensor vinculi* takes part in the trial, he too, may appeal, but he has no obligation to do so.[44]

The purpose of the judicial investigation in the process for declaration of death is the establishment of the material truth. For this reason, even though the *defensor vinculi* is not present to oppose the granting of the declaration, the judge will not be satisfied merely with the evidence presented by the parties, but will, when necessary, bring in evidence against giving the declaration.[45]

The argument sometimes advanced that, where the evidence is mainly based on presumptions, cases of this kind should be handled in judicial procedure, does not seem justified. As has

[40] Canon 1576, § 2.

[41] S. C. C., 14 dec. 1889—*ASS,* XXII (1889-1890), 546; the presence of the *defensor vinculi* is required only in cases involving the bond of marriage.—Canons 1586, 1967.

[42] *Instructio Austriaca,* n. 247—*Collectio Lacensis,* V, 1314; S. C. C., 14 dec. 1889. Cf. Péries, *Code de Procédure Canonique dans les Causes Matrimoniales* (Paris, 1894), n. 102; Lanier, *Guide Pratique de la Procédure Matrimoniale en Droit Canonique* (Paris: Pierre Tequi, 1927), p. 9.

[43] Cf. canon 1587, § 1.

[44] S. C. C., 14 dec. 1889; S. C. S. Off., 8 maii 1891, ad III—*Fontes,* n. 1135.

[45] "Ex quo id saltem fluere videtur, quaestionem huiusmodi spectare potius ad officium nobile iudicis, quam ad forum contentiosum."—S. C. C., 14 dec. 1889. "Illud autem est speciale in morte probanda ut testes non citata parte, sed ex mero iudicis officio examinari possint."—Sanchez, *De Sancto Matrimonii Sacramento,* lib. II, disp. 46, n. 8. Cf. canons 1618, 1619..

already been seen,[46] this process is primarily an administrative one, which, however, may be handled in a judicial manner, if the Ordinary deems it advisable.

Kaas, in his excellent work on this process, argues strongly for the use of judicial procedure in these cases. Among the reasons he adduces for his opinion, the following are worthy of mention: (1) The terminology of general regulations of the various instructions of the Holy See imply the use of judicial procedure. (2) The importance of safeguarding the bond of marriage, although in a technical sense this question is not one respecting the *vinculum.* (3) The bishop's authorization, under canon 1576, § 2, to place important cases before a tribunal of three or five judges. He attempts at some length to demonstrate that the question of declaration of death meets the requirements of this canon. (4) A judicial procedure will be fairer and more impartial than an administrative one, and will make a better impression on the parties in the event that their petition is not granted.[47]

In answer to this line of argument it may be stated, that if the Holy See desired that this process should ordinarily be handled as a judicial procedure, it would have been included in the judicial processes mentioned in the Fourth Book of the Code. Besides, canon 1576, § 2, does not refer to the question of whether judicial or administrative procedure should be used, but to the option given the Ordinary of using three or five judges in a judicial procedure where but one judge is required. It may be added that the Holy See has permitted the administrative settlement by the Ordinary of difficult cases of presumed death.[48]

[46] Cf. *supra,* p. 43.

[47] Kaas, *Kriegsverschollenheit und Wiederverheiratung,* pp. 87-88. Wanenmacher (*Canonical Evidence in Marriage Cases* [Philadelphia: The Dolphin Press, 1935], n. 4) holds that judicial procedure should be used in cases of presumed death.

[48] " . . . saltem summarie et exraiudicialiter . . . "—S. C. S. Off., 17 apr. 1887—*AER,* VIII (1893), 144; cf also S. C..C., *in Papien. Matrimonii,* 12 dec. 1733 et 27 febr. 1734—*Thesaurus Resolutionum S. C. C.,* VI (1733-1734), 181, 215, where the final decision of the Congregation was *"arbitrio episcopi."*

Article IV. The Pastor's Place in the Investigation

A. *The Pastor's Obligation to Refer the Case to the Ordinary*

A very important point with regard to the process for proof of death of a husband or wife with regard to freedom to contract a second marriage concerns the part played by the pastor. This can be a matter of considerable importance in practice. When a case is presented to the pastor involving the proof of death of a first spouse of one of the parties contemplating a new marriage, the question may arise: If the pastor is morally certain that the spouse in question is really dead, is it necessary for him to present the case to the Ordinary?

Some of the older authors, notably Schmalzgrueber, Reiffenstuel and Pirhing, held that in such a case it was not necessary for the pastor to send the case to the Ordinary if he had moral certainty that the first spouse was dead, even if his certainty was based on circumstantial evidence.[40]

Canon 1031, referring to the preliminary investigation of marriage in general, states:

> § 1. Exorto dubio de existentia alicuius impedimenti:
> n. 1. Parochus rem accuratius investiget, interrogando sub iuramento duos saltem testes fide dignos, dummodo ne agatur de impedimento ex cuius notitia infamia partibus oriatur, et, si necesse fuerit, ipsas quoque partes; . . .
> § 3. Matrimonio ne assistat, inconsulto Ordinario, si dubium adhuc superesse prudenter iudicaverit.

[40] "Quando habetur certitudo moralis de morte coniugis, prout habetur per modos, seu probationes a nn. 10 usque ad 15 allegatos [the proofs referred to included those from documents, witnesses of various kinds, and circumstantial evidence], potest Parochus nulla petita licentia Ordinarii, et absque illius praescitu Marimonio assistere, eoque novos coniuges licite copulare . . . quia in casu, quo moralis certitudo adest, ipsa Iura . . . facultatem nubendi tribuunt, consequenter licentia Ordinarii non amplius est necessaria. Accedit, quod 'eum, qui iam certus est, certiorari ulterius non oporteat," c. *eum, qui* de Reg. Iuris in 6."—Reiffenstuel, lib. IV, tit. 21, n. 19. The same opinion is expressed by Schmalzgrueber, lib. IV, tit. 21, n. 19. Pirhing (lib. IV, tit. 1, § 5, n. 2) while holding the same view adds a note of caution: "longe tamen tutius est, ut res ad Ordinarium deferatur."

Canon 1069, § 2, states that it is not allowable to contract a second marriage until it has been established "legitime et certo" that the first has been dissolved. The question to be settled here, is: when may the pastor's decision suffice for the *legitimate* establishment of the death of a first spouse?

All authors are agreed that the pastor can proceed and need not consult the Ordinary, when he has personal knowledge of the death of the party (if he assisted at the funeral, for example), or if the record of the death appears on the parish books, or if he has secured an authentic document certifying the death of the party concerned.[50] They feel that the rule of law (Reg. 31, R. J., in VI°) applies to this case: "Eum, qui certus est, certiorari ulterius non oportet."

The great majority of authors, both before the Code and after, hold that, when the pastor does not have personal knowledge or authentic documentation of the death of a first spouse, the question must be presented to the Ordinary for settlement and it is beyond the province of the pastor to reach a decision.[51]

However, when two eye-witnesses testify to the death of the

[50] Giraldi (*Expositio Iuris Pontificii,* II, Sectio 656), an eighteenth century canonist, held that when a person had died in a distant land, the pastor should consult the ordinary, even though an authentic document certifying death was at hand. The authors are agreed that this requirement is too severe. Cf. Gasparri, *De Matrimonio* (ed. tertia, Romae: 1904), I, n. 723; Wernz, *Ius Decretalium* (2. ed., Romae, 1908-1913), IV, n. 371, nota 67.

[51] Kutschker, *Eherect,* I, 233; Scherer, *Handbuch des Kirchenrechtes* (Graz und Leipzig, 1886-1898), II, 354; Santi-Leitner, *Praelectiones Iuris Canonici* (Ratisbonae, 1905), IV, 350; Wernz, *Ius Decretalium,* IV, n. 371; Augustine, *A Commentary on the New Code of Canon Law* (4. ed., St. Louis: B. Herder, 1921-1929), V, 178; Chelodi, *Ius Matrimoniale* (4. ed., Tridenti: Libreria Moderna Editrice A. Ardesi, 1937), n. 78; Fourneret, *Le Marriage Chrétien* (4. ed., Paris: Gabriel Beauchesne, 1925), p. 191; Gasparri, *De Matrimonio* (ed. nova), n. 562; Haring, *Grundzüge des katholischen Kirchenrechtes* (3. ed., Graz: Ulrich Mosers Buchhandlung, 1924), II, 494; Kaas, *Kriegsverschollenheit und Wiederverheiratung,* p. 84; Lanier, *Procédure Matrimoniale,* p. 9; Noldin-Schmitt, *Summa Theologiae Moralis* (25. ed., Oeniponte: Fel. Rauch, 1938), III, n. 573; Triebs, *Handbuch des kanonischen Eherechts,* p. 310.

first spouse, there are several authors who would permit a pastor to solve a case of this kind without consulting the Ordinary.[52] Cappello goes even farther and permits the pastor to proceed without consulting the Ordinary when the death of the first spouse is certified by but one eye-witness.[53] One or the other author would permit the pastor to assist at a second marriage without consulting the Ordinary, even when his moral certitude of the death of the first spouse was formed from circumstantial evidence only.[54]

To sum up the teaching of the authors on the question: It is certain that, when the pastor possesses an authentic document testifying to the death of the first spouse, he can permit a second marriage without consulting the Ordinary. It is equally certain that unless there are two eye-witnesses who testify to the death of

[52] Feije, *De Impedimentis et Dispensationibus Matrimonialibus* (3. ed., *Lovanii,* 1885), n. 445; Vromant, *De Matrimonio* (Louvain: Museum Lessianum, 1931), n. 44. Donovan (*The Pastor's Obligation in Pre-Nuptial Investigation* [The Catholic University of America, Canon Law Studies, n. 115, Washington; The Catholic University of America, 1938], p. 179) upholds this view, although on page 135 of the same work he states that, where the dissolution of the previous bond of marriage by death cannot be proved by an authentic death certificate, the pastor should turn the case over to the diocesan Curia. Genicot-Salsmans (*Institutiones Theologiae Moralis* [11. ed., Bruxelles: Alb. Dewit, 1927], II, 444) and Payen (*De Matrimonio in Missionibus ac Potissimum in Sinis Tractatus Practicus et Casus* [2. ed., Zi-ka-wei: T'ou-sè-wè, 1935-1936], I, n. 1050) seem also to hold that the pastor could handle the case himself, when he has the testimony of two eyewitnesses to the death of the first spouse. However, Payen *(ibidem)* holds the stricter view in practice: "In Sinis, ut plurimum, dubium prudens solo documento authentico removetur. Deficiente igitur huiusmodi documento, in usu consulendus est Ordinarius, cuius est declarare utrum habeatur vera certitudo moralis.", Cf. also Payen, *op. cit.,* I, n. 408.

[53] *De Matrimonio,* n. 396.

[54] Pighi, *Cursus Theologiae Moralis* (4. ed., Veronae: Sorores Cinquetti Filiae Felicis, 1926), IV, n. 499; Vlaming (*Praelectiones Iuris Matrimonii* [3. ed., Bussum in Hollandia, 1919], I, n. 281) would seem to hold this opinion, although he states that as a rule the Ordinary should be consulted, unless moral certitude has been obtained by at least the testimony of one witness.

the first spouse, the pastor is severely bound in conscience to consult the Ordinary. Although there is some probability to the opinion that, when there are two eye-witnesses the pastor may proceed without consulting the Ordinary, it is far more probable that in this case also the case should be turned over to the Ordinary for settlement.

For the following reasons it is maintained here that, except in the case where the pastor has personal knowledge of the death of the first spouse or an authentic death certificate, all cases involving the proof of death of a husband or wife belong to the competence of the Ordinary:

(1) The preponderant opinion of canonists, especially since such authorities as Wernz and Gasparri hold this view, strongly supports the contention that cases of this kind should be handled by the Ordinary.

(2) There is a great difference between the preliminary investigation into the presence or absence of impediments in general, and the establishment of the dissolution of *ligamen*. For in the latter case the presumption holds for the first marriage, and the first marriage is in possession until its dissolution has been proved.[55] That special care is to be taken in such cases, over and above the precautions required in the ordinary pre-nuptial investigation, is indicated by the numerous instructions of the Holy See on this particular point.

(3) All the pertinent instructions of the Holy See on the proof of death of a spouse refer to the Ordinary. For example, the authoritative instruction of 1868 is directed especially to the Ordinary, and nothing is said concerning the pastor's part in the process.

(4) The process itself is one of such difficulty that it is entirely beyond the capability of the pastor's office as such to handle it. The sifting of evidence, the question of the credibility of witnesses, etc., clearly demand a quasi-judicial process, which pertains to the Ordinary, and not to the pastor.

From what has been said, it would seem that a bishop would

[55] Canon 1014.

be justified in making it a rule in his diocese, that, except in the case where an authentic certificate of death is available, cases involving the proof of death of a husband or wife should be turned over to the Ordinary for settlement. Such a provision has been made by the provincial Council of Venice, held in 1925.[56]

With regard to soldiers missing in the Civil War (1861-1865), the Second Plenary Council of Baltimore reserved the handling of such cases to the Ordinary.[57]

B. *In Danger of Death*

Canon 1019, § 2, states with regard to the proof of freedom to marry:

> In periculo mortis, si aliae probationes haberi nequeant, sufficit, nisi contraria adsint indicia, affirmatio iurata contrahentium se baptizatos fuisse et nullo detineri impedimento.

It may be asked, could the provisions of this canon be used in a case involving the proof of death of a former spouse? It would seem that it may be used by the pastor in two cases: a) when the parties themselves had actual, personal knowledge of the death of the first spouse; b) when the parties had received documentary evidence of the death of the spouse of one of them, for instance, official notification from the government of his death in war, or official notification of his death in another country received from the civil or ecclesiastical authorities. Of course all the conditions mentioned in the canon would have to be present, (1) danger of death, (2) the impossibility of obtaining further

[56] "Quando agitur de feminis, quae praesumuntur viduae, quia scilicet earum mariti dicuntur obiisse, nec tamen de eorum morte ullum habeatur authenticum documentum, si novum petant matrimonium contrahere, certitudinis suffragia, quae haberi possint, undique pro viribus colligantur a parocho, et ad loci Ordinarium, cui in his casibus recurrendum est, transmittantur."—d. 269, quoted by Cerato, *Matrimonium a codice I. C. integre Desumptum* (4. ed., Patavii, Libr. Gregoriana edidit typis seminarii, 1927), p. 99.

[57] "Constet itaque, antequam novae nuptiae licite iniri possint, requiri certam prioris conjugis mortis cognitionem quae nonnisi ab Ordinario, omnibus bene perpensis, probari jure debet."—*Concilii Plenarii Baltimorensis II, Acta et Decreta,* n. 328.

proofs, and (3) the absence of reasons for the pastor to doubt their word and of circumstances that would lead him to have a well founded doubt of the couple's veracity.

It would seem that in such circumstances, when there was not time to consult the Ordinary, the pastor could be satisfied with the sworn statement of the parties that they were baptized, and were not bound by any impediments, specifically that the first spouse was dead.[58]

This canon certainly could not be used when there was any doubt of the death of the first spouse, or any question of presumed death.

Article V. Proof of Death in Cases Wherein the Missing Person is an Infidel

The case may arise when a Catholic wishes to marry a non-Catholic, concerning the death of whose first spouse it is impossible to obtain moral certitude. If both parties to the first marriage were not baptized, it will be possible to make use of the Pauline Privilege.[59] It will be necessary to obtain a dispensation from the interpellations from the Holy See, unless the Ordinary has the faculty to dispense.[60] When one of the parties to the first marriage was baptized and the other unbaptized, it may be possible to obtain a dissolution of the natural bond in *favorem fidei* from the Holy See.[61]

[58] Cf. Vromant, *De Matrimonio,* n. 40. Vromant here notes that in missionary countries in a case of this kind the details of the death and funeral of the deceased spouse, given by the surviving party, will often be of more value than an oath in establishing certainty.

[59] Canons 1120-1127. Cf. Payen, *De Matrimonio,* I, nn. 398-399, nn. 443-444. Cf. also S. C. S. Off., 31 maii 1865, ad 3, 4, 7—*Fontes,* n. 983.

[60] Canon 1121.

[61] S. C. S. Off., 5 nov. 1924—*AER,* LXXII (1925), 188. Cf. Cappello, *De Matrimonio,* n. 792; Ayrinhac-Lydon, *Marriage Legislation in the New Code of Canon Law* (2. ed., New York: Benziger Brothers, 1938), p. 322.

CHAPTER V

PROOF OF DEATH BY DOCUMENTS AND WITNESSES

ARTICLE I. PROOF BY DOCUMENTS

The first kind of proof to be sought with regard to the death of a husband or wife is documentary evidence. Only when it is absolutely impossible to obtain documentary pròof, is it permissible to proceed with the other proofs outlined in the instruction of 1868.[1]

An ecclesiastical certificate of death should be obtained if possible. Certificates of this kind may be obtained from parish registers, the registers of Catholic hospitals, the records of Catholic cemeteries, or from the records kept by Catholic chaplains in time of war. If it proves impossible to obtain an ecclesiastical certificate of death, a certificate from the civil authorites will suffice. A certficate of death from the military authorities in the case of soldiers will also be acceptable, taking into account certain precautions which will be seen later.[2]

With regard to the documentary proof of death, the regulations of canon law with regard to the place and value of documents

[1] S. C. S. Off., 12 iun. 1822—*Collectio Lacensis,* III, 557; S. C. S. Off., instr. 13 maii 1868, nn. 2-3—*Fontes,* n. 1002; S. C. de Prop. Fide, instr. a. 1883, n. 42—*Fontes,* n. 4901; S. C. S. Off., instr. 22 aug. 1890, n. 11—*Fontes,* n. 1128.

[2] Et si respondeat mortuos fuisse in aliquo hospitali, vel vidisse sepeliri in certa ecclesia, vel occasione militiae sepultos fuisse a militibus, non detur licentia contrahendi nisi prius recepto testimonio authentico a rectore hospitalis in quo praedicti decesserunt, vel a rectore ecclesiae in qua humata fuerunt eorum cadavera, vel si fieri potest, a duce illius cohortis in qua descriptus erat miles." S. C. S. Off., instr. 21 aug. 1670, n. 11—*Fontes,* n. 742.

"Hinc ad praescriptum eorumdem sacrorum Canonum, documentum authenticum obitus diligenti studio exquiri omnino debet; exaratum scilicet ex regestis paroeciae, vel xenedochii, vel militiae, vel etiam, si haberi nequeat ab auctoritate ecclesiastica, a gubernio civili loci in quo, ut supponitur, persona obierit."—S. C. S. Off., instr. 13 maii 1868.

as evidence in trials should be kept in mind.[3] Documents may be either public or private. A document is public if it emanates from public authority, while a private document is one that depends upon private authority for its efficacy. Records of death kept in the official registers of the Curia, parish or religious institute, are considered public ecclesiastical documents; similarly the written certificates taken from these original records and issued by the pastors, Ordinaries, or ecclesiastical notaries, as well as authentic copies of them.[4]

Records copied from parish registers should be exactly as the originals; nowadays, as a rule, excerpts from the parish registers are made on printed forms which may not always be in verbal agreement with the original records. Nevertheless, when such forms are filled out completely, and attested by signature and seal, they constitute authentic copies, even though they are not word for word transcripts from the register.[5] Although assistant pastors *per se* have no power to issue authentic certificates of death, it would seem that this power can be delegated to them explicitly or implicity, so that in practice certificates issued by them can be considered as authentic.[6]

Public civil documents are those which are considered such by the laws of the respective country.[7] A document of death issued by a non-Catholic church can be considered as a proof, but has only the value to be attributed to private documents. If it were the only documentary proof of the death of a spouse, it would have great value.

A public document is *authentic* if issued by the proper public official. That a copy be considered authentic it is necessary that it be signed either with the signature of the persons in charge

[3] Canons 1812-1824.

[4] Canon 1813.

[5] Cappello, *De Matrimonio,* n. 149; De Smet, *De Sponsalibus et Matrimonio,* n. 678; Wanenmacher, *Canonical Evidence in Marriage Cases,* n. 339.

[6] Augustine, *A Commentary on Canon Law,* VII, 257; Wanenmacher, *Canonical Evidence in Marriage Cases,* n. 340.

[7] Canon 1813, § 2.

of the archives where the originals are kept or with the signature of an ecclesiastical notary; a seal should always be affixed.[8] There would seem to be nothing to prevent the use of photostatic copies provided that they are duly signed and attested.[9] A document is *genuine* if it was written or signed by the person whose signature is affixed. Public documents, whether ecclesiastical or civil, are presumed to be genuine until the contrary is proved.[10]

Public documents give full proof concerning those things which are directly and principally affirmed in them.[11] Thus a death record gives full proof of the fact, time and cause of death, but not of other facts that might be mentioned in it, such as the date of the person's birth, whether he was married or single, and so on. It should be noted that documents do not have probative force unless they are originals or duly authenticated copies.[12]

When confronted with a document certifying to the death of a husband or wife, the pastor should examine it carefully, to see whether it is a public or a private document, whether it is authentic and genuine or not. If there are any erasures, changes or additions to the document, he should examine it with special care. If these were obviously made by the official drawing up the document, and it is a public document, these changes will not interfere with the value of the document. If there is any doubt as to the accuracy of the document, or any question of its having been tampered with, it will be best for the pastor to consult with the person who drew up the certificate. If this is impossible the pastor should refer the matter to the Ordinary.[13]

[8] S. C. de Sacr., instr. 15 aug. 1936, art. 159—*AAS,* XXVIII (1936), 313-361.

[9] Doheny, *Canonical Procedure in Matrimonial Cases,* p. 279.

[10] Canon 1814.

[11] Canon 1816.

[12] Canon 1819.

[13] In a case brought before the Sacred Congregation of the Council in 1733 (S. C. C., *in Papien. Matrimonii,* 12 dec. 1733 et 27 febr. 1734—*Thesaurus Resolutionum S. C. C.,* VI [1733-1734], 181, 215) the Bishop of Pavia declined to accept a certificate of death, issued by an army chaplain in the case of an army surgeon, for the following reasons: 1) It was not certain that the individual mentioned in the death certificate

Public civil documents testifying to a person's death should as a rule be accepted as full proof of the person's death,[14] unless there is some reason to doubt their credibility. An example of the latter took place in connection with the earthquake in Sicily and Calabria, December 28, 1908, when the Holy See declined to accept the certificates of death issued by the Italian government, on the ground that they were mere declarations of death based on the fact that the individuals were missing after the disaster.[15]

More care will need to be exercised when a certificate is issued by the military authorities in connection with the death of a soldier in battle. Not infrequently the basis for the certificate of death will be the more or less trustworthy statements of comrades of the deceased soldier. When the trying conditions encountered in time of war are taken into consideration, it is not surprising that mistakes will sometimes be made by the military authorities, and that occasionally soldiers taken prisoner by the enemy will be erroneously listed among the dead. In most cases of this kind the error will be corrected by word being received from the soldier in captivity before the question of a new marriage comes up.

This does not mean that the pastor should view every military certificate of death with suspicion. As a rule they can be accepted as full proof of the person's death. During the World War great care was taken by the army authorities of all countries, through the use of tags and the like, to make the identification of the soldiers who fell in battle as accurate as was humanly possible. If, however, the pastor has some reason to doubt the fact of the soldier's death as stated in a military certificate, the

was the same person who had married the petitioner. 2) Suspicion was cast on the authenticity and genuineness of the document due to a discrepancy in dates; the certificate stated that the man was buried on the day before he died. 3) The certificate was not issued under the authority of the Ordinary, nor were there witnesses to testify to its authenticity. 4) A man (possibly a handwriting expert) whom the Bishop had investigate the case, came to the conclusion that the certificate was false.

[14] Canons 1814, 1816.

[15] S. C. de Sacr., 12 mart. 1910—*AAS,* II (1910), 196.

question should be sent to the Ordinary for settlement.[16] During time of war, if the wife of a soldier officially certified as dead wished to marry very shortly after receipt of the notification of death, an especially careful investigation would seem in order.

When there is a public authentic certificate of death, either from the civil or the ecclesiastical authorities, the pastor may proceed without consulting the Ordinary. If there is any question of the authenticity or genuineness of the document, or if the document is a private one, the case should be turned over to the Ordinary for settlement.[17] When the question of the correctness or trustworthiness of a certificate of death is presented to the Ordinary, he should have someone examine the original or procure a photostatic copy of it.[18]

The pastor must be careful to check the death certificate with the certificate of the first marriage, so as to make sure that it is the spouse in question for whom the certificate of death has been issued.

It should be remembered that it is in the mind of the Holy See that, when certificates are obtained from foreign countries, they should be handled through the Ordinaries of the respective dioceses.[19]

When the pastor encounters a case of proof of death which must be sent to the Ordinary for settlement, he should assiduously gather all the private documents which will be of value in helping the Ordinary reach a decision on the case. Letters received from the missing spouse will be of the greatest importance, especially to show the attitude of the absent person towards his wife and family, and the reasons or lack thereof which might lead the missing person intentionally to disappear.[20]

[16] Kaas, *Kriegsverschollenheit und Wiederverheiratung,* p. 93; Schlenz, "Wiederverehelichung auf Grund der Todeserklärung"—*AKKR,* XCVIII (1918), 382; Schaaf, "Proof of Death of Husband or Wife"—*AER,* LXXXIX (1933), 282.

[17] Cf. *supra,* p. 55.

[18] Canon 1821.

[19] S. C. de Sacr., 4 iul. 1921—*AAS,* XIII (1921), 348.

[20] S. C. de Sacr., 19 ian. 1917—*Fontes,* n. 2117. Cf. *infra,* p. 87..

ARTICLE II. THE CHURCH'S ATTITUDE TOWARDS THE CIVIL DECLARATION OF DEATH

What attitude should the Ordinary take when confronted with a declaration by the civil authorities of the death of a missing person? Here two extremes are to be avoided.

In the first place the civil declaration of death cannot be accepted by the ecclesiastical authorities as full proof of death.[21] For the primary end of the State in declaring a missing person dead is different from that of the Church. The Church is first of all anxious to protect the unity and indissolubility of marriage; the State is only secondarily interested in the question from the standpoint of marriage; its primary interest is in the economic side of the problem, especially with regard to the disposal of the missing person's property. The State places much emphasis on the lapse of the statutory period; this is of importance for the Church only as one of the corroborating circumstances which lead to moral certainty of the death of the person. In such cases merely to rely on the result of the civil investigation is to expose the sacrament of matrimony to the danger of abuse.

On the other hand the civil declaration of death can prove of great value to the ecclesiastical authorities, and should be taken into consideration by the Ordinary in arriving at a decision on the question.[22] It must not be forgotten that the civil authori-

21 "Hinc quaeritur: 1. Utrum provisiones legis civilis de absentibus coniugibus, locum certitudinis moralis de eorum morte tenere possint, ac consequenter utrum derelicti coniuges, perfectis et impletis istis provisionibus, aliud matrimonium legitime contrahere valeant. . . . R. 1. Iuxta expositum, Negative, et expendendos esse casus particulares ab ipso Vic. Ap. iuxta Instructionem quae eidem communicetur." S. C. S. Off., 28 iun. 1865 (response to a query presented by the Vicar Apostolic of Pondicherry, India)—*Fontes,* n. 984.

22 "Argumenta etiam desumi possunt ex actis a Tribunali civili confectis et deinde super illis, instituto examine, ubi nihil contrarium reperiatur, ab Ecclesiastica potestate, ferri debet sententia, qua declaratur satis constare de obitu personae de cuius existentia inquiritur." S. C. S. Off., 6 febr. 1861 (1863)—quoted in S. C. S. Off., 8 maii 1891 (date here is given as 1863)—*Fontes,* n. 1135, and in S. C. de Sacr., 16 dec. 1910 (date here is given as 1861)—*Fontes,* n. 2104.

ties have at their disposal much greater means than the Church for obtaining certainty of the death of a person—the police, missing person's bureau, official records of various kinds. At least the grounds should be considered upon which the civil officials arrived at their decision, and it will be for the Ordinary to decide whether he believes that this provided a compelling basis of proof.

The value of the civil declaration for the ecclesiastical authorities will depend on a number of circumstances; sometimes it will have been made with great care and after a thorough investigation, at other times it will have been handed down with entirely too much haste. For this reason, in all valuations of the results of State investigations, the Ordinary has to examine them conscientiously, and through his own investigations as much as possible to complete them, so that in this way he may obtain at least moral certainty of the death of the missing person.[23]

In the United States, the civil declaration of death has but little relation to the question of remarriage.[24] Its most important place will be in property cases, especially in the settling of estates of missing persons. When someone has an interest in opposing the granting of the declaration, e.g., an insurance company, the decision will naturally be reached after more deliberation, and will for that reason be of greater value to the ecclesiastical authorities.

The same general rule (for the evaluation of civil declarations of death) applies to the declaration of death of military bureaus in the case of missing soldiers. It is noteworthy that the Sacred

" . . . nihil impedimento erit, quominus in huiusmodi iudicio instituendo utaris actibus factis a Foris saecularibus et a Consistoriis acatholicis tamquam probationibus extraiudicialibus." Instruction of Pius VI to an Austrian bishop—Kutschker, *Eherect,* I, 234.

[23] S. C. de Sacr., 12 mart. 1910—*AAS,* II (1910), 196; Schlenz, "Wiederverehelichung auf Grund der Todeserklärung"—*AKKR,* XCVIII (1918), 66; Lehmkuhl, "Wiederverheiratung nach längerem Vermisstsein des totgeglaubten Gatten"—*TPQ,* LXX (1917), 113-117; Kaas, *Kriegsverschollenheit und Wiederverheiratung,* pp. 77-82; Linneborn, *Grundriss des Eherechts* (5. ed., Paderborn: Ferdinand Schöningh, 1933), p. 235.

[24] Cf. *infra,* p. 127.

Congregation of the Sacraments attached great importance to the official decision of a Russian military tribunal in the case of a soldier missing after the battle of Mukden in the Russo-Japanese war.[25]

ARTICLE III. PROOF OF DEATH BY WITNESSES

A. *Witnesses in General*

Although the process for proof of death of a husband or wife will practically always be handled administratively, it seems fitting, nevertheless, that the Ordinary in this process follow the general regulations for witnesses in trials as laid down in canons 1754-1791. Before going into the question of the proof of death by witnesses, a short summary of the teaching of these canons will be given here.

Exempt from the obligation of testifying are those to whom the knowledge of the facts of a case has been revealed while acting in their professional capacity, and is therefore a professional secret, e.g., priests (in those matters that have been revealed to them outside sacramental confession by reason of their sacred ministry), civil magistrates, physicians, nurses, lawyers, notaries.[26]

Those who have not attained the age of puberty and persons who are feeble-minded are looked upon as unfit (*non idonei*) to give testimony.[27] The age of puberty is fourteen for boys, twelve for girls.[28] Among those considered as feeble-minded are the insane, idiots, imbeciles, and probably the lower grades of morons.[29] The following are considered suspected (*suspecti*)

[25] "Et in praesenti casu militis Iacob Ondzul, quamvis acta non exarata fuerint a Tribunali civili, attentis tamen circumstantiis, peculiari vi pollet documentum de morte Iacobi, quod edidit specialis sectio pro colligendis notitiis de occisis et vulneratis militibus in bello cum Iaponia." S. C. de Sacr., 12 dec. 1910—*Fontes,* n. 2104.

[26] Canon 1755.

[27] Canon 1757, § 1.

[28] Canon 88, § 2.

[29] Whalen, *The Value of Testimonial Evidence in Matrimonial Procedure* (The Catholic University of America, Canon Law Studies, n. 99, Washington: The Catholic University of America, 1935), p. 112.

witnesses: (a) Excommunicated persons, perjurers, and legally infamous persons, after a declaratory or condemnatory sentence has been issued against them. (b) Those who are so depraved and perverse in morals that they cannot be considered worthy of credence. (c) Public and implacable enemies of the party concerned.[30] Unfit and suspected witnesses may be permitted by the judge to testify, but their testimony has only the value of an indicative and adminicular proof. Such witnesses are usually not put under oath.[31] Disqualified entirely from being witnesses are the following: (a) Those who are parties in the case or take the place of the parties, such as guardians in the case of a ward; the judge and his assistants, the advocate of the parties in the case, and all others who are assisting or have assisted the parties in the case. (b) Priests in all matters of which they have obtained knowledge from sacramental confession, even if they have been freed from the obligation of the seal; nothing that has been heard by anyone in connection with confession, can be brought forward as evidence, not even as an indication of the truth. (c) Close relatives of the parties.[32] However, in matrimonial cases close relatives are permitted to testify, and their testimony is often the most valuable of all.[33] The admission or rejection of volunteer witnesses (who appear of their own initiative) is left to the prudent judgment of the judge.[34] It may be said that in general the volunteer witness is looked upon with suspicion in canon law.[35]

[30] Canon 1757, § 2.

[31] Canon 1758.

[32] Canon 1757, § 3.

[33] Canon 1974.

[34] Canon 1760. The canon is much more lenient in this regard than some of the pre-Code instructions of the Holy See: " . . . an ad examen accesserit sponte, vel requisitus; si dixerit accessisse sponte a nemine requisitum, dimittatur, quia praesumitur mendax." S. C. S. Off., 21 aug. 1670, n. 4—*Fontes,* n. 742; "Animadvertat iudex, ne admittat eos qui sponte ad examen accesserint, quia mendaces praesumuntur." S. C. de Prop. Fide, instr. a. 1883, n. 43—*Fontes,* n. 4901; "Si dicat se accessisse sponte a nemine requisitum, dimittatur, quia praesumatur mendax." S. C. S. Off., 22 aug. 1890, n. 10—*Fontes,* n. 1128.

[35] Whalen, *The Value of Testimonial Evidence in Matrimonial Procedure,* p. 139.

The testimony of witnesses is to be given under oath.[36] This is required specifically for the process of proof of death by the instruction of 1868.[37] The oath should be administered to the witnesses before they give their testimony.

The witnesses should be examined separately.[38] The questions to be proposed to the witness are of two kinds, general and particular. The purpose of the former is to ascertain general information about the witness, such as his full name, his birth, age, religion, profession, domicile (including his address), whatever connection or relationship exists between him and the parties in the case. The particular questions are asked to elicit the truth about the facts upon which the case hinges. The witness should be examined very closely as to the source of his knowledge, so as to find out whence, how and when (*unde, quomodo, quando*) his knowledge of the facts was acquired; specifically whether he was an eye-witness or has obtained his information from others.[39] The questions put to the witness should be brief, not complex, not tricky, not captious, not leading questions, nor offensive in any way, and should be relevant to the case under discussion.[40] In addition the questions should be adapted to the intelligence of the persons being examined and expressed in the ordinary language of the people.[41]

It would seem that in the administrative process for proof of death the judicial practice with regard to the interrogatories could well be followed in all particulars. Thus the interrogatories should be prepared in advance, in this case by the Ordinary or his delegate, since the *defensor vinculi* will not be present. The testimony of the witness is to be given orally, and should be written down by the notary in the identical language used by the witness. When the examination is finished, his testimony should

[36] Canons 1767-1769.

[37] S. C. S. Off., 13 maii 1868, n. 3—*Fontes,* n. 1002.

[38] Canon 1772.

[39] Canon 1774.

[40] Canon 1775.

[41] S. C. de Sacr., instr. 15 aug. 1936, art. 102—*AAS,* XXVIII (1936), 313-361.

be read to the witness, and the opportunity given him of adding, suppressing, correcting, or changing what has been written. The testimony should then be signed by the witness himself, the judge (in this case the Ordinary or his delegate) and the notary.[42]

In evaluating the testimony of witnesses, the judge should keep before his mind (a) the status and character of the witness, his honesty, and whether he holds a responsible position; (b) whether he is testifying from personal knowledge, or whether his testimony is based on common opinion, rumor, or hearsay; (c) whether the witness is consistent; or inconsistent, uncertain and vacillating; (d) finally, whether his testimony is corroborated by other witnesses or whether it stands alone.[43] If the witnesses disagree, the judge must decide whether their statements are mutually contradictory, or whether only different or supplementary.[44] The testimony of one witness does not give full proof, that is, moral certitude, unless he is a qualified witness testifying concerning those things performed in his offical capacity;[45] for example, a pastor would be a qualified witness with regard to the baptisms and marriages at which he officiated. Ordinarily, moral certitude and therefore sufficient proof will be obtained, if two or three persons, absolutely worthy of credence and in strict agreement with one another, under oath give testimony which is based on personal knowledge of the fact in question. The judge can demand more complete proof if he judges it necessary in view of the exceptional importance of the matter, or if there are indications which give rise to some doubt about the truth of an assertion.[46] Testimony of the religious character, the probity and the credibility of all witnesses should be demanded. The greater the degree in which the witness is shown to possess these qualities, the more credence is to be given to his testimony.[47]

[42] Canons 1777-1780.
[43] Canon 1789.
[44] Canon 1790.
[45] Canon 1791, § 1.
[46] Canon 1791, § 2.
[47] S.C. de Sacr., instr. 15 aug. 1936, art. 138—*AAS,* XXVIII (1936), 313-361.

From the practice of the Sacred Congregation of the Sacraments in handling cases of the proof of death of a husband or wife, it is clear that the surviving spouse may, and in fact sometimes should, be called as a witness. In two recent decisions the most important evidence offered was that presented in the testimony of the surviving spouses.[48] It will usually be a wise procedure to take the testimony of the surviving spouse early in the process, as he or she will best be able to shed light on the date of and the reasons for the absence of the missing spouse. The surviving spouse will also be able to testify concerning any news received from the missing person. The motives which lead the living party to believe that the missing spouse is dead will also be of value in arriving at a decision.[49]

B. *Two Eye-Witnesses*

Full proof (moral certitude) of the death of a missing husband or wife can be obtained from the testimony of two eye-witnesses.[50] As eye-witnesses may be considered not only those who were present at the person's death or saw him lying dead, but also those who were present at his funeral or burial, provided that the circumstances in this last case were such as to leave no doubt as to who was being buried.[51]

48 S. C. de Sacr., 25 iun. 1915—*Fontes,* n. 2112; S. C. de Sacr., 19 ian. 1917—*Fontes,* n. 2117. Cf. also S. C. S. Off., 18 iul. 1900—*AER,* XXIV (1901), 387; *AKKR,* LXXXI (1901), 345; S. C. de Sacr., 25 febr. 1916—*Fontes,* n. 2115.

49 Whalen, *The Value of Testimonial Evidence in Matrimonial Procedure,* p. 260.

50 "Porro quandoque hoc documentum haberi nequit; quo casu testium depositionibus supplendeum erit. Testes vero duo saltem esse debent, iurati, fide digni, et qui de facto proprio deponant an defunctum cognoverint, ac sint inter se concordes quoad locum et causam obitus aliasque substantiales circumstantias. Qui insuper, si defuncti propinqui sint, aut socii itineris, industriae, vel etiam militiae, eo magis plurimi faciendum erit illorum testimonium." S. C. S. Off., instr. 13 maii 1868, n. 3—*Fontes,* n. 1002.

51 "Si de obitu eius deponant duo testes de visu, et attestantur, se interfuisse illius morti, sepulturae, exequiis, aut vidisse ipsius sepulchrum, vel consanguineos pulla veste indutos, et audisse talem maritum lugeri. . . . "

The witnesses should give their testimony under oath. In this process it will be enough to administer the oath before the taking of testimony.

The credibility of the witnesses must be established. To establish the credibility of the witnesses, the Ordinary should call other witnesses, for instance, the pastor and other reputable persons in the community, to ascertain the witnesses' reputation for veracity, their character in general, and the common repute of their trustworthiness. It will also be advisable by prudent questioning to find out if the witnesses have any ulterior motive in testifying to the death of the person in question, if they stand to gain by the establishment of the death of the missing spouse, if any pressure was brought to bear on them by the relatives or consort of the absent person, or if any inducement was offered to them in regard to their testimony.[52] The witnesses must be in agreement concerning the time, place and cause of the death of the person, and other substantial circumstances, for example, the place where the person is buried.[53] It must also be established that the witnesses were sufficiently acquainted with the deceased to identify him, and to be certain that the person was the spouse in question.[54]

The greatest value will be placed on the testimony of witnesses who are near relatives of the alleged deceased, as they will be in a better position to give reliable testimony of a fact of this nature.[55]

—Schmalzgrueber, lib. IV, tit. 21, n. 11. Cf. also Reiffenstuel, lib. IV, tit. 21, n. 12.

[52] S. C. S. Off., instr. 22 aug. 1890, n. 10—*Fontes,* n. 1128.

[53] S. C. S. Off., instr. 13 maii 1868, n. 3; S. C. S. Off., instr. 22 aug. 1890, n. 11; cf. canon 1791.

[54] "Similiter advertat [iudex], non esse admittendos testes qui personas, de quibus agitur, plene non cognoscant."—S. C. de Prop. Fide, instr. a. 1883, n. 43. Cf. S. C. S. Off., instr. 13 maii 1868, n. 3; S. C. de Sacr., 18 dec. 1914, ad I—*Fontes,* n. 2109.

[55] "Pro testibus in hac materia recipiantur magis consanguinei, quam extranei, quia praesumuntur melius informati."—S. C. S. Off., instr. 21 aug. 1670. "Qui insuper, si defuncti propinqui sint . . . eo magis plurimi faciendum erit illorum testimonium."—S. C. S. Off., instr. 13 maii 1868, n. 3. "Ad testimonium ferendum in hac materia . . . recipiuntur magis consanguinei, nempe parentes, fratres, sorores, etc., quam externi, quia praesumuntur melius informati."—S. C. S. Off., instr. 22 aug. 1890, n. 4.

If the missing person died while on a journey, great value will be placed on the testimony of his fellow travellers; fellow workmen will be important witnesses when a person died in a foreign land; for a soldier missing or killed in war the testimony of his comrades will be the most valuable evidence.[56]

Vromant notes that in missionary countries the agreement of witnesses concerning the details of the death and funeral of the alleged deceased, e.g., the number of mourners, musicians, etc., will be of the greatest value in arriving at moral certainty of the death of the person.[57]

The following questions, based on the instructions of 1868 and 1883, will be of assistance in preparing interrogatories for eyewitnesses in cases of proof of death:

Have they known the alleged deceased well? Were they present at his death or did they see him dead subsequently? At what time and at what place did he die? Under what circumstances did he die? Before his death did he give them any kind of message? What, in their opinion, was the cause of death? Where is his grave to be found? Can they name persons who have knowledge of the facts of the death, whether from their own observation, or from hearsay knowledge. Can they name persons of whom it is at least probable, that they can testify something concerning the facts of his death? [58]

C. *One Witness*

In canon law the testimony of one witness does not suffice for full proof.[59] However, the Holy See, under certain conditions, permits the acceptance of the testimony of one witness as full proof

[56] "Qui insuper, si defuncti propinqui sint, aut socii itineris, industriae, vel etiam militiae, eo magis plurimi faciendum erit illorum testimonium." —S. C. S. Off., instr. 13 maii 1868, n. 3.

[57] *De Matrimonio*, n. 40. Payen (*De Matrimonio,* I, n. 404) warns the judge in missionary countries to beware of the witnesses who give many minute details of the death of the party. He also states that in China a witness can be presumed mendacious who spontaneously calls on God's name to bolster the truth of his assertion.

[58] Kaas, *Kriegsverschollenheit und Wiederverheiratung,* p. 95.

[59] Canon 1791.

of the death of a husband or wife, because of the Church's reluctance to force a person whose spouse is dead to lead a celibate life[60] The instruction of 1868 permits the use of one witness under the following conditions:

(1) It must be impossible to obtain more than one witness.

(2) He must possess the qualities required for the witnesses in n. 3 of the instruction, that is, he must be an eye-witness, absolutely trustworthy, and must have known the alleged deceased so as to have been able to identify him.[61]

(3) He must be a witness to whom no exception can be taken, that is, he must possess all the requirements of a reliable witness in the highest degree.

(4) His testimony must be supported by other weighty adminicular evidence.[62] If it is altogether *(omnio)* impossible to gather this additional evidence, the testimony of one witness will still be acceptable, provided that it is absolutely certain that there is nothing in his testimony which does not possess the appearance of truth by itself and with relation to the other circumstances of the case. In practice it will rarely happen that there is a reliable

60 "Interdum unus tantum testis examinandus reperitur, et licet ab omni iure testimonium unius ad plene probandum non admittatur, attamen ne coniux alias nuptias inire peroptans vitam coelibem agere cogatur, etiam unius testimonium absolute non respuit Suprema Congr. in dirimendis huiusmodi casibus, dummodo ille testis, recensitis conditionibus sit praeditus, nulli exceptioni obnoxius, ac praeterea eius depositio aliis gravibus adminiculis fulciatur: sique alia extrinseca adminicula colligi omnino nequeant, hoc tamen certum sit, nihil in eius testimonio reperiri quod non sit congruum atque omnino verisimile." S. C. S. Off., instr. 13 maii 1868, n. 4—*Fontes,* n. 1002.

" . . . sed vel testem omni exceptione maiorem adesse oportet, qui vidisse se mortuum priorem coniugem sacramenti religione confirmet . . . " S. C. de Prop. Fide, instr. a. 1792—*Fontes,* n. 4632.

61 Cf. *supra,* p. 71.

62 "Concordari sententia utraque [of those who say one witness would suffice and of those who deny this] potest, si dicatur, unius quidem, etiam fide digni hominis testimonio mortem sufficienter non probari, eam tamen moraliter certam effici, quando cum eius depositione concurrunt circumstantiae, vel coniecturae aliquae ex enarratis, vel aliae similes, et de his legitime constat."—Schmalzgrueber, lib. IV, tit, 21, n. 14.

eye-witness to the death of a person, and at the same time no circumstantial evidence available.[63] It should be noted that one eye-witness, no matter how reliable, will not be able to overcome strong circumstantial evidence against the fact of the death of a husband or wife.

It may be of some value to discuss briefly several cases in which the Sacred Congregations dealt with instances of proof of death wherein there was but one eye-witness, and to note carefully how the norms laid down by the Holy Office for the evaluation of the testimony of one witness are carried out in practice.

In 1733 the Sacred Congregation of the Council refused to permit remarriage to a widow in a case in which the bishop had declined to accept a certificate of death as authentic and genuine. In 1734 the case was presented again, and new evidence was introduced. The testimony was offered of a man who served in the same legion as the alleged deceased and knew the latter well, heard him often lament the fact that he had left his wife in Milan, saw him gravely ill and then lying dead, and was present at his burial. The testimony of this witness of itself sounded very accurate and trustworthy. He confirmed the fact that the priest was actually the chaplain of the corps who signed the death certificate. In addition the pastor of this witness testified that he was reliable and of good character. The Congregation left the final decision to the bishop.[64]

In 1860 there was presented to the Sacred Congregation of the Council a case in which the question at issue was the proof of death of a man who allegedly was killed during a riot. There was one eye-witness who saw his dead body being taken away for burial. In addition two other persons had seen him enter a

[63] "Primam [the opinion which holds that one eye-witness suffices for proof of death] admitterem casu quo coniux obierit in loco ita distanti, ut facile nequeant aliae probationes haberi; tunc enim satis erit nuncius, et ita unus testis, considerata qualitate personae, et ut verisimilia dicat."—Sanchez, *De Sancto Matrimonii Sacramento,* lib. II, disp. 46, n. 12.

[64] S. C. C., *in Papien. Matrimonii,* 12 dec. 1733 et 27 febr. 1734—*Thesaurus Resolutionum S. C. C.*, VI (1733-1734), 181, 215. Cf. *supra,* p. 62, note 13.

building where he was in danger of losing his life; two additional witnesses saw him lying gravely wounded. The witnesses were all trustworthy and were well acquainted with the person in question. Their testimony was in substantial agreement, and there was no reason to suspect conspiracy. Besides, although diligent efforts had been made to locate the alleged deceased, nothing had been heard of him for twelve years. There was no reason, outside of death, to account for his disappearance: he was not sought by the government for his part in the disturbance; his home life had been happy. The Sacred Congregation decided that the death of the man was established with moral certainty, and his wife was permitted to remarry.[65]

The Sacred Congregation of the Sacraments gave permission in 1914 to a woman to contract a new marriage upon the following evidence of death of her husband: (a) There was one eye-witness who saw the person in question lying dead on the occasion of an epidemic. It was established that the witness was entirely reliable. (b) There were four hearsay witnesses, whose testimonies agreed with one another, and with the otherwise known facts of the case, and with the testimony of the one eye-witness. (c) Witnesses testified to the common opinion *(fama)* in the region that the spouse in question was dead. (d) The man was missing for 25 years; he had gone to a country where many of his fellow countrymen had emigrated, and where they were accustomed to stay for two or three years and then return to their homeland. (e) Thorough investigations were made, and no trace of the missing spouse was found. (f) The woman and her new "husband" were considered by all in the community as man and wife. (g) With regard to the fact that nothing was found in the parish or civil records concerning the death of this man, it was brought out that at the time of the epidemic during which he was alleged to have died, many people were buried without record being made, or at least without their names being recorded.[66]

In the last two cases, in which a favorable decision was given

[65] S. C. C., *in Mediolanen. Matrimonii,* 22 sept. 1860—Pallottini, "Matrimonium," § 14, nn. 36-41, 58-64.

[66] S. C. de Sacr., 18 dec. 1914—*Fontes,* n. 2109.

by the Congregations, the strength of the adminicular evidence supporting the testimony of the one eye-witness is noteworthy.

D. *Hearsay Witnesses*

When the testimony of eye-witnesses is not available, full proof of the death of a spouse may be obtained from trustworthy hearsay witnesses (*testes de auditu*).[67] Four conditions must be fulfilled before hearsay witnesses will be acceptable for the proof of death of a missing spouse:

(1) It must be impossible to obtain the testimony of eye-witnesses to the death of the person. This will happen, either because the eye-witnesses are dead, or absent, or for some other good reason cannot be examined. If the eye-witnesses are absent, efforts should be made to have their testimony taken by the Ordinary of the place where they reside and forwarded to the Ordinary who is conducting the investigation.[68] It may be impossible to obtain the testimony of living eye-witnesses for various reasons: their whereabouts may be unknown; they may have become insane; it may be impossible to reach them, for example, because the country where they reside is at war with the country where the investigation is being conducted.

[67] "Contigit etiam ut testes omnimoda fide digni testificentur se tempore non suspecto mortem coniugis ex aliorum attestatione audivisse, isti autem vel quia absentes, vel quia obierint vel aliam ob quamcumque rationabilem causam examinari nequeunt; tunc dicta ex alieno ore, quatenus omnibus aliis in casu concurrentibus circumstantiis, aut saltem urgentibus respondeant, satis esse censentur pro sequutae mortis prudenti iudicio." S. C. S. Off., instr. 13 maii 1868, n. 5—*Fontes,* n. 1002.

"Etiam contigit, ut testium fide dignorum probe informatorum dicta, tempore non suspecto ab aliis percepta fuerint; testes autem immediati vel morte vel absentia, aut alia de causa audiri nequeant, habeantur vero dicta testium de alieno dicto deponentium, qui tamen omnibus pensatis prudenti mortis secutae iudicio satis esse censeantur." S. C. S. Off., instr. 12 iun. 1822—*Collectio Lacensis,* III, 557.

" . . . argumentum desumi potest [ad mortem prioris coniugis probandam] ex depositione testium fidem merentium, si . . . mortem illius asseruerint ex auditu, dummodo non ex vaga aliqua relatione, sed a personis minime suspectis proprias informationes se hausisse testentur." S. C. de Prop. Fide, instr. a. 1883, n. 43—*Fontes,* n. 4901.

[68] Cf. canon 1770, § 2, nn. 3-4.

(2) The hearsay witnesses must have obtained the information concerning the death of the spouse from actual eye-witnesses of the event. From the language of the instruction of 1868 (*ex attestatione aliorum audivisse*) it would seem that the testimony of the hearsay witnesses must be based on the statements of at least two eye-witnesses.

(3) The testimony of the hearsay witnesses must have the appearance of truth, so that it conforms to at least the most important circumstances of the case.

(4) The hearsay witnesses must have obtained their information *tempore non suspecto.* When the hearsay witnesses are relatives, friends or even acquaintances, of the surviving spouse, the *tempus suspectum* would begin when the surviving spouse decided to remarry and became aware, even though vaguely, that it would be necessary to establish with certainty the death of the first spouse. When the witnesses and their informants are strangers to the surviving spouse, the *tempus suspectum,* so far as their testimony is concerned, would begin from the time that they realized that the establishment of the death of the missing person was necessary for the legal remarriage of the surviving spouse.[69] If these conditions are all present the testimony of the hearsay witnesses will suffice for the obtaining of moral certitude and the declaration of death of the missing person.

None of the published decisions of the Holy See on the question of proof of death depended exclusively or even primarily on the testimony of hearsay witnesses, although in several cases their testimony was important in a supporting rôle. For example, an important factor in leading the Sacred Congregation of the Sacraments in 1914 to permit a woman, whose husband had long been missing, to remarry, was the testimony of their son, that he was long ago told by two witnesses (no longer available)

[69] " . . . tempore non suspecto . . . eo nempe tempore, quando de hac quaestione introducenda ne cogitabatur quidem, nec aliae suberant rationes veritatem occultandi aut falsum proferendi." *Regulae Servandae in Processibus super Matrimonio Rato et Non Consummato,* S. C. de Sacr., 7 maii 1923, n. 70—*AAS,* XV (1923), 392. Cf. Doheny, *Canonical Procedure in Matrimonial Cases,* p. 190.

that his father had died at a certain time and a certain place. One of these witnesses, a reliable and trustworthy individual, had told the son that his father went out in a boat to swim, that he did not appear again, and his clothes were found on the bridge where he left them.[70]

The following questions based on the instructions of 1868 and 1883 [71] will be of help in preparing interrogatories for the examination of hearsay witnesses: Through what persons have they obtained knowledge of the alleged death of the missing person? When and under what conditions did they obtain this information? What is their belief of the credibility of their informants? When is the missing person said to have died? Where? Under what circumstances? Do they know whether the death of the missing person was known to their informants through their own observation or through the communication of others? Had their informants perhaps special grounds for circulating the news of the death of the missing person? Were they financially or otherwise interested in the death of the missing person? When did they discover that the spouse of the missing person was interested in establishing his death? Way there anything to indicate that their informants were aware of the surviving spouse's intentions in this regard?

E. *The Suppletory Oath*

There does not seem to be any place for the suppletory oath in the process for proof of death of a husband or wife. The suppletory oath is to be administered to the parties in a case when only half proof has been offered in a trial and no other

[70] S.C. de Sacr., 28 nov. 1914—*Fontes,* n. 2109. Other decisions where the testimony of hearsay witnesses was of importance were S. C. C., *in Mediolanen. Matrimonii,* 22 sept. 1860—Pallottini, "Matrimonium," § 14, nn. 36-41, 58-64; S.C. de Sacr., 18 dec. 1914—*Fontes,* n. 2109; cf. *supra,* p. 76.

[71] "Ab illis vero qui ex aliorum relatione deponunt, erit quoque inquirendum a quibus tales hauserint notitias; a quo tempore fama de morte vulgari coeperit, et quid ipsi sentiant de probitate et credulitate eorum qui primitus de re ista sunt loquuti; utrum isti peculiarem aliquam rationem habuerint aut habere potuerint ut talem notitiam evulgarent."—S.C. de Prop. Fide, instr. a. 1883, n. 43.

means of proof are available.[72] The suppletory oath is especially to be used when facts which pertain to the civil or religious status of a party cannot otherwise be ascertained.[73] It can therefore be used to furnish evidence that a person is unmarried.[74] The suppletory oath is not applicable to cases of proof of death of a spouse for two reasons: (1) The suppletory oath must embrace some right, object or fact proper to the litigant to whom the oath is tendered. Hence the facts sworn to must fall within the scope of the knowledge of the person taking the oath.[75] It will rarely or ever happen that the case will arise in which the surviving party has personal knowledge of the death of the other spouse and wherein other proofs are not available. (2) The suppletory oath is excluded in trials in which the disputed fact is of very great importance.[76] The fact is obviously of such a nature in a case wherein the death of the spouse of a first marriage is in question; for the first marriage is in possession until it has been definitely proved dissolved by death.[77]

[72] Canon 1829.

[73] Canon 1830, § 1.

[74] Moriarty, *Oaths in Ecclesiastical Courts* (The Catholic University of America, Canon Law Studies, n. 110, Washington: The Catholic University of America, 1937), pp. 66-80; Coronata, *Institutiones Iuris Canonici,* nn. 1360-1363.

[75] Canon 1830, § 2.

[76] Canon 1830, § 2.

[77] Wernz-Vidal, *Ius Canonicum,* V, n. 255, nota 53; De Becker, *De Matrimonio Praelectiones Canonicae* (ed. nova, Louvain; Fr. Ceuterick, 1931), p. 43; Triebs, *Handbuch des kanonischen Eherechts,* p. 313.

Chapter VI

PRESUMED DEATH

Article I. Presumptions

It will not infrequently happen that it will be impossible to produce witnesses of any kind to the death of a missing person. In such cases it may be possible to obtain enough evidence of other kinds to give rise to a presumption of death sufficiently weighty to furnish moral certainty of the death of the person in question. When such a case arises a thorough investigation should precede the opening of the process, to make sure that all the evidence bearing on the death of the missing person has been gathered.. Proof of death may be obtained from conjectures, presumptions, indications and circumstances of various kinds, which taken together will give rise to moral certainty of the death of the husband or wife in question. The decision, as to whether or not these various factors taken together are sufficient in a particular case to establish a presumption of death so strong as to cause moral certainty, is left to the judge, who in the administrative process will be the Ordinary or his delegate.[1]

[1] "Verum haud semel experientia compertum habetur, quod ne unus quidem reperiatur testis, qualis supra adstruitur. Hoc in casu probatio obitus ex coniecturis, praesumptionibus, indiciis, et adiunctis quibuscumque, sedula certe et admodum cauta investigatione curanda erit, ita nimirum ut pluribus hinc inde collectis, eorumque natura perpensa, prout scilicet urgentiora vel leviora sunt, seu propiore vel remotiore nexu cum veritate mortis coniunguntur, inde prudentis viri iudicium ad eamdem mortem affirmandam probabilitate maxima, seu morali certitudine promoveri possit. Quapropter quandonam in singulis casibus habeatur ex huiusmodi coniecturis simul coniunctis iusta probatio, id prudenti relinquendum est iudicis arbitrio; heic tamen non abs re erit plures indicare fontes ex quibus illae sive urgentiores, sive etiam leviores colligi et haberi possint." S. C. S. Off., instr. 13 maii 1868, n. 6—*Fontes,* n. 1002.

" . . . aut tales coniecturae de ilius interitu intervenire debent, quae prudentem virum ita plane esse morali quadam certitudine persuadeant." S. C. de Prop. Fide. instr. a. 1792—*Fontes,* n. 4632.

"Verum in tantis, quibus saepe huiusmodi mortis probationes premuntur

A presumption is a probable inference about an uncertain matter. When a presumption is expressly stated and admitted in law it is called a legal presumption (*praesumptio iuris*); when it is not necessarily indicated in law, but is deduced from the circumstances of the case by the judge himself, it is called a personal presumption (*praesumptio hominis*).[2] The presumption here discussed is of the latter kind, that is, it must be formed by the judge himself from the evidence presented. It should be kept in mind that recourse to proof by presumption is never permitted until every effort has been made to locate documentary or testimonial proofs. Only when these are unavailable or insufficient are presumptions to be used. It must also be remembered that a presumption will not suffice for full proof unless it attains to moral certainty.[3]

The necessity of a thorough investigation in cases of presumed death cannot be stressed enough. In practically every case sub-

difficultatibus, S. Congregatio nullam respuit, quae aliquid ad fidem faciendam valeat, ut perspice possit, an pluribus quandoque concurrentibus, quae seorsim certitudinem sufficientem parere nequeunt, omnia tamen simul iuncta hanc efficiant." S. C. S. Off., instr. 12 iun. 1822—*Collectio Lacensis,* III, 557.

"Verum quandoque contigit, ut nullus testis haberi queat. Tunc coniecturae, praesumptiones, indicia colligenda. Haec potissimum ex ipsis coniugibus desumenda." S. C. S. Off., 6 febr. 1863, quoted in S. C. S. off., 8 maii 1891—*Fontes,* n. 1135. In a decision of the Sacred Congregation of the Sacraments (16 dec. 1910—*Fontes,* n. 2104) the date of this instruction is given as February 6, 1861.

" . . . a novo matrimonio prohibere, nisi forte ex pluribus saltem coniecturis (quae sin minus singulae, at certe simul coniunctae certitudinem moralem pariant) demonstrari possit legitimum eorum coniugem mortem vere obiisse." S. C. S. Off., 31 maii 1865—*Fontes,* n. 983.

"Quod si testes sive de visu, sive de auditu haberi non poterunt, considerandae erunt circumstantiae omnes in facto concurrentes, et diligenter ponderandae, ut videatur, utrum ex illarum complexu exurgere possit moralis illa certitudo quae necessaria est ut iudicium proferatur." S. C. de Prop. Fide, instr. a. 1883, n. 43—*Fontes,* n. 4901.

[2] Canon 1825, § 1. Cf. Manning, *Presumptions of Law in Marriage Cases* (The Catholic University of America, Canon Law Studies, n. 94, Washington: The Catholic University of America, 1935), p. 9.

[3] Wanenmacher, *Canonical Evidence in Marriage Cases,* n. 384.

mitted to the Holy See the fact that a most thorough investigation had failed to produce documentary or testimonial proof of the death of the missing person was adduced. It may safely be said that the Holy See will not grant a declaration of death in a case of this kind, until every avenue of investigation has been explored in so far as this is reasonably possible. It is likewise true that many cases which look hopeless will prove possible of solution if the interested parties and the diocesan authorities are prepared to launch a thorough investigation. It does not seem either just or fair for diocesan officials to dismiss petitions of this kind before such an exhaustive investigation has been made.

Nowadays it is not too difficult to make thorough investigations. The care with which records are kept by the civil authorities in modern times facilitates inquiries of this kind. There will be found bureaus in all states and large cities which check up on missing persons. The police will often be helpful. In our own country it will be of advantage to consult Social Security records, old age pension lists, census reports, bureaus of vital statistics, and the Federal Bureau of Investigation in Washington. With regard to those who served in the army or navy, the pension and Veterans' Bureau lists will be of value; the fact as to whether or not a former soldier claimed his bonus will serve as an indication of whether he is alive or dead. The instruction of 1868 suggests the use of newspapers wherever possible.[4] If the missing person is a Catholic, inquiry should be made of the ecclesiastical authorities of the place where he was last heard of.

Before proceeding farther, it will be well to affirm once again that long absence of itself is not sufficient to give rise to a reasonable presumption of death.[5] It may well be that the absent per-

[4] "Tandem, si opus fuerit, praetereunda non erit investigatio per publicas ephemerides, datis directori omnibus necessariis personae indiciis, nisi ob speciales circumstantias saniori ac prudentiori consiliio aliter censeatur." S. C. S. Off., instr. 13 maii 1868, n. 9. In a case decided by the Sacred Congregation of the Sacraments (25 iun. 1915—*Fontes*, n. 2112) notices were placed in language newspapers read by the people of the race of the missing person in America.

[5] "Cum de coniugis morte quaestio instituitur, notandum primo loco

son has reasons for disappearing and for creating the appearance of death.[6] However, in certain circumstances long and unexplained absence can serve as an important indication in helping to establish the proof of death, especially in the case of an individual of upright character, who is known to be devoted to his wife and family and has no special reason for disappearing.

The first and necessary basis for an ecclesiastical declaration of death in such cases is the fact that for a long time there has arrived no news of the life or death of the person concerning whose death an official declaration is sought. Among the published decisions of the Holy See there is only one case in which the time elapsed after the missing person's disappearance is under five years,[7] and in most of the cases the time elapsed was considerably longer than five years.

Three elements will usually be required to establish a presumption of death: (1) the first, negative, i.e., absence of reasons for disappearing, (2) the second, positive, i.e., some place or event which would be likely to cause death, a battle, a shipwreck, an earthquake, and (3) the third, corroborative, i.e., the other

quod argumentum a sola ipsius absentia quantacumque (licet a legibus civilibus fere ubique admittatur) a sacris canonibus minime sufficiens ad iustam probationem habetur." —S. C. S. Off., instr. 13 maii 1868, n. 1. Cf. c. 19, X, *de sponsalibus et matrimoniis,* IV, 1; S. C. de Prop. Fide, 21 apr. 1788—*Fontes,* n. 4620; S. C. de Prop. Fide, instr. a. 1792—*Fontes,* n. 4632.

" . . . ex longa coniugis absentia non resultat certitudo de eius obitu, sed tantum incertitudo." —Sanchez, *De Sancto Matrimonii Sacramento,* lib. II, disp. 46, n. 1.

[6] "Quidam putabant, matrimonium quaestionis ex alio capite ratihaberi posse; cum nempe maritus longiore tempore absens auctoritate regia citatus non comparuerit, moralem fere certitudinem de eius morte praesto esse. Neque id satis argumenti est ad mortem comprobandam. Nam quod vir non comparuerit, non magis mors in causa esse potuit, quam eius contumacia." Letter of Pius VI to the Archbishop of Prague, July 11, 1789 — Kutschker, *Eherecht,* I, 218. This letter is quoted in S. C. S. Off., instr. 13 maii 1868, n. 1.

[7] S. C. S. Off., 20 iul. 1898 (Adua case)—*ASS,* XXXI (1898-1899), 252. The three shortest periods of absence were all in cases of soldiers missing after a battle. Cf. *infra,* p. 93.

circumstances of the case must be such as to bolster the first two. However, all three will not be found in every case, and favorable decisions have been granted by the Holy See where one or the other was lacking.

The first point to be established refers to the person of the missing individual.[8] It will be necessary to examine into his background to see if from his previous life light can be shed on the question as to whether or not he would be likely to leave home and absent himself intentionally. This information can be obtained from the testimony of relatives, friends, neighbors and associates of both spouses. Inquiry should be made into the life of the missing person to discover if he was a man of good moral character, if he was attentive to his religious duties. One of the most important points to establish will be the missing person's relations with his wife and family: was he devoted to his wife and family, was his married life happy, were there any serious disagreements between husband and wife? It will also be important to look into the financial affairs of the absent person: was he comfortably fixed, did he own property, did he have expectations of being left money by relatives or others? In the case of a business man it will be wise to check on his business affairs, to see if there might be some irregularities in his accounts which might have tempted him to flee and absent himself. It will also be helpful to know if the absent person left home with the consent of his family. It will always be important to find out exactly why the missing person left home.[9]

[8] "Itaque in primis illae praesumptiones investigandae erunt quae personam ipsius asserti defuncti respiciunt, quaeque profecto facile haberi poterunt a coniunctis, amicis, vicinis, et quoquo modo notis utriusque coniugis." —S. C. S. Off., instr. 13 maii 1868, n. 7.

[9] S. C. S. Off., instr. 13 maii 1868, n. 7; S. C. de Prop. Fide, instr. a. 1883, n. 43. The importance of trying to learn whether a missing person had any reason for disappearing and giving the impression that he is dead, may be gathered from the following recent news items from the daily press:

"Los Angeles. Nov. 14. Declared legally dead since his disappearance from Pittsburgh 14 years ago, Davis R. MacDonald, sought for years by Government investigators, has been found—a prisoner in the Los

If the result of these investigations shows that the man in question was of general good character, and had no apparent reason for wishing to disappear, a firm basis is established in building up the presumption of death. It should be noted, however, that even if the investigations turn out otherwise, and it is found that the individual in question was not reputable, did not get along with his wife and family, or had other reasons for leaving home, it will still be possible to establish reasonable presumption of death. However, the other evidence will have to be of great strength to overcome the weakness in the points mentioned. As a matter of fact, there are several cases in which the Holy See gave favorable decisions although the individuals had left home in disagreement with their spouses.[10] In other

Angeles county jail. Arrested on a forgery charge under the name of John Edgar Davis, the alias he has been using since he vanished, MacDonald, former Pittsburgh broker, was identified through fingerprints by agents of the Federal Bureau of Investigation. MacDonald who is 45, disappeared February 13, 1924, after a suicide note had been found in his clothes, placed near a river. The note said he was going to drown himself. Seven years after his disappearance, MacDonald's first wife, now Mrs. Clara Margaret O'Brien, received a settlement on her suit to recover $10,000 on a Government war risk insurance policy, in addition to an undetermined amount on two other policies he held. Since remarried and the father of two children by his second wife, MacDonald said he had heard only indirectly of his first wife. Regarding his disappearance, MacDonald said he was 'in a jam' and thought there was but one way out. However, he lost his nerve, he said."—*Washington Times,* November 14, 1938.

"Willimantic, Conn. July 31. Nearly a year after his overturned canoe was found in Willimantic River and he was mourned as dead by his wife and 4-year old son, Joseph G. Beaulieu came home. He explained that after the boat capsized he decided to go to Canada and it was not until recently he heard his family and friends believed him drowned."—*Pittsburgh Press,* July 31, 1939.

[10] S. C. de Sacr., 18 dec. 1914—*Fontes,* n. 2109; S. C. de Sacr., 29 apr. 1915—*Fontes,* n. 2111. Favorable decisions were granted in two other cases (S. C. S. Off., 13 sept. 1871—*AKKR,* XXVII [1872], III; S. C. de Sacr., 19 ian. 1917—*Fontes,* n. 2117) in which men deserted their wives, but subsequently in letters they wrote home expressed sorrow for their conduct and indicated their intention of returning to their families.

cases the Holy See has given a declaration of death in instances where individuals had reasons for leaving the country and when it was to their advantage not to return.[11]

It will be of value to find out the age of the person who disappeared.[12] In cases of long-continued disappearance, the advanced age of the missing person will be an important point in arriving at a presumption of death, especially if it is linked with poor health or depraved morals. In several cases decided by the Holy See the advanced age of the absent spouse (if he were still living) was an important factor in arriving at moral certainty of his death.[13] Inquiry should be made concerning the health of the missing person,[14] as poor health in connection with advanced years will lead to a conjecture of death.

Great attention should be paid to any news that has been heard from the missing person, either from himself before his disappearance, or from others after his disappearance. If any letters sent to the missing spouse were returned, the observation made by the postal authorities may be of some value. Special inquiry should be made as to the tenor of any letters that were received from him, since from these it will be possible to obtain indications of his attitude towards his wife and family, of his intention of returning, of events or conditions in the place where he was living which might provide a clue to the possibility of death.[15]

[11] S. C. S. Off., 18 iul. 1900—*AER,* XXIV (1900), 387; S. C. de Sacr., 28 nov. 1914—*Fontes,* n. 2109; S. C. de Sacr., 25 iun. 1915—*Fontes,* n. 2112.

[12] S. C. S. Off., instr. 13 maii 1868, n. 7; S. C. de Prop. Fide, instr. a. 1883, n. 43—*Fontes,* N. 4901.

[13] S. C. S. Off., 18 iul. 1900—*AER,* XXIV (1900), 387; S. C. de Sacr., 28 nov. 1914—*Fontes,* n. 2109; S. C. de Sacr., 29 apr. 1915—*Fontes,* n. 2111.

[14] S. C. S. Off., instr. 13 maii 1868, n. 7; S. C. de Prop. Fide, instr. a. 1883, n. 43 The poor health of the missing party was one of the factors which received weighty consideration from the Sacred Congregation of the Sacraments in issuing a declaration of death on June 25, 1915. Cf. *Fontes,* n. 2112.

[15] "An aliquando et quo loco scripserit, et num suam voluntatem quamprimum redeundi aperuerit, aliaque huius generis indicia colligantur." S. C. S. Off., instr. 13 maii 1868., n. 7—*Fontes,* n. 1002.

The sudden cessation of correspondence, without apparent reason, by a man who was devoted to his family and who wrote to his family at regular intervals will be a strong presumption in favor of his death.[16] Several cases have been decided by the Holy See in which the sudden cessation of correspondence on the part of an absent spouse was given weighty consideration in arriving at a presumption of death.[17]

Conditions prevalent in the country to which the missing person went may throw light on the possibility of his death. If a person went to a place which had an unhealthy climate and where disease was very prevalent, or if he went to a region where conditions were disturbed through economic unrest, revolution, earthquake, and the like, the chances of his death would be considerably increased.[18] For example, the last letter received from a soldier in Cuba stated that he was in the hospital suffering from a serious pulmonary disease, and that yellow fever was sweeping the country; the latter fact was established from other sources, and had a strong bearing on the eventual favorable decision by the Sacred Congregation of the Sacraments.[19]

The instruction of 1868 gives a list of questions which should be asked in connection with shipwreck cases. A careful inves-

[16] "Haec cognosci vel deduci poterunt ex benevolis aut contrariis relationibus, quae vel coniuges habuerunt inter se, durante eorum contubernio, vel ille qui discessit continuavit cum altero coniuge sive per litteras sive per nuncios: si enim constiterit, ad tempus talem epistolarum sive relationum consuetudinem adfuisse, et postea cessasse, quin cessationis causa aut ratio appareat, gravis de morte obita praesumptio habebitur; si e contra constiterit eum qui discessit numquam epistolarum commercium habuisse cum sua familia, aut cum propinquis et amicis, indicium mere negativum nullam probationem facere poterit." S.C. de Prop. Fide, instr. a. 1883, n. 43—*Fontes,* n. 4901.

[17] S.C.S. Off., 13 sept. 1871—*AKKR,* XXVII (1872), 111; S.C.S. Off., 18 iul. 1900—*AER,* XXIV (1901), 387; S. C. de Sacr., 25 iun. 1915—*Fontes,* n. 2112; S.C. de Sacr., 25 febr. 1916—*Fontes,* n. 2115; S.C. de Sacr., 19 ian. 1917—*Fontes* n. 2117; S.C. de Sacr., 18 nov. 1920—*AAS,* XIV (1922), 95.

[18] S.C.S. Off., instr. 13 maii 1868, n. 7—*Fontes,* n. 1002; S.C. de Prop. Fide, instr. a. 1883, n. 43—*Fontes,* n. 4901.

[19] S.C. de Sacr., 19 ian. 1917—*Fontes,* n. 2117.

tigation should be made in connection with the following points: From what port did the ship sail, what was its destination; what was the name of the ship, the name of the company owning the ship, who was the captain? How can it be proved that the person in question was aboard the ship? Did the ship meet with disaster? Is there any possibility that the person in question might have left the ship before the disaster took place? What special circumstances are there to indicate that the spouse in question was lost in the disaster? Special pains should be taken to locate any of the passengers or crew who became acquainted with the missing person, and to take their testimony as to what happened to him. If there were no survivors to the disaster, it will be important to discover whether or not the insurance company made compensation for the missing ship. The records of the ship company should be carefully studied to find out what information they have about the missing person.[20]

There is one published decision of the Holy See which refers to the proof of death of a person allegedly lost in a sea disaster.[21] A summary of the case will serve to show the practice of the Holy See in such cases. A German left his home in 1855 after domestic quarrels with his wife and went to Australia. After some time he began to write to his relatives. From 1861 on his letters indicated that he was sorry for his desertion of his wife and was anxious for a reconciliation with her and with his family. In January 1865 he wrote that he intended to leave Australia and expected to arrive home in May of that year. At the beginning of April of the same year a ship sailed from Brisbane, Australia, for England. Some distance out at sea the ship caught fire; of eighty persons who left the ship in four lifeboats, none ever reappeared; eighteen persons who stayed on the ship

[20] "Si maritimum iter fuerit aggressus, sedula investigatio fiat a quo portu discesserit; quinam fuerint itineris socii; quo se contulerit; quod nomen navis quam conscendit; quis eiusdem navis gubernator; an naufragium fecerit; an societas, quae navis cautionem forsan dedit, pretium eius solverit; aliaeque circumstantiae, si quae sint, diligenter perpendantur." S. C. S. Off., instr. 13 maii 1868, n. 7—*Fontes,* n. 1002.

[21] S. C. S. Off., 13 sept. 1871—*AKKR,* XXVII (1872), 111.

were saved. From various circumstances it was indicated that the man in question had embarked on the ship. A relative of his father testified that the missing individual went aboard the ship; the *"restaurateur"* testified that a man with a name sounding like the German's was on the ship; a name on the passenger list closely resembled his, although there was a slight variation in the first name. The civil court declared the missing person dead in 1870. In the same year the ecclesiastical court of first instance of Trier declined to issue a declaration of death. The case was appealed to the court of the archdiocese of Cologne, which overruled the court of first instance and granted permission to the wife to remarry. The case was appealed again by the *defensor vinculi* of Cologne to the Holy Office, which upheld the court of second instance and permitted remarriage. A period of six years elapsed between the disappearance and permission to remarry.

The aftermath of war and of persecution often gives rise to unsettled conditions as a result of which many wives and husbands are separated, never to hear of each other again. An example of such a situation is to be found in Poland in 1939 when the country was divided between Russia and Germany. Hundreds of thousands of people have been driven from their homes and forced to settle in other districts, and husbands and wives have been forcibly separated. It is easy to see how as a result of such a situation many spouses will lose all trace of their partners. The Holy See has pointed out on more than one occasion that the existence of such conditions in a certain district can by no means be taken as full proof of the death of a person missing as a result of the troubled times.[22]

[22] "Allatae a vobis calamitates belli, famis, captivitatis, aliaeque huius generis, quae vastitatem regioni ac plurimis interitum attulerunt, non tanti ponderis sunt ut viris aut mulieribus, qui coniuges amiserunt, passim permitti possit novas nuptias appetere.' S. C. de Prop. Fide, instr. a. 1792 —*Fontes,* n. 4632.

"Inter fideles sunt qui, tempore famis vel persecutionis separati ab uxoribus, illas amiserunt, et post plurium annorum perquisitionem minime invenerunt, nec ullam quidem notitiam utrum eae vivant an mortuae sint

The same attitude has been taken by the Holy See with regard to disasters arising from natural disturbances, earthquakes, floods, famines and the like. The mere fact that a person is missing after such a disaster will not suffice for a reasonable presumption of death. The attitude of the Holy See in this regard is evident from its handling of cases arising out of the earthquake of 1908 in Sicily and Calabria. In the early morning of December 28, 1908, one of the most disastrous earthquakes ever recorded totally destroyed the city of Messina, Sicily; the damage was done chiefly by the shock and by the fires which broke out afterwards. The seismic wave which followed did vast damage elsewhere along the strait between Sicily and Calabria, and especially at Reggio, Calabria, ten miles across the strait from Messina. This city likewise was almost totally destroyed. In the city of Messina about 84,000 persons, half the population of the city, perished. In Reggio, over 35,000 persons lost their lives.

On January 18, 1909, the Sacred Congregation of the Sacraments sent to the Archbishops of the two cities instructions as to the procedure to be followed with regard to the establishment of freedom to marry, stating specifically with regard to cases where the death of a husband or wife could not be proved by documentary evidence, that the provisions of the instruction of 1868 were to be followed. During the next year and a half the two Archbishops sent several letters to the Sacred Congregation asking for special rules to govern the cases of proof of death arising out of the earthquake; their concern was due mainly to their desire to validate the many illicit unions that followed in the wake of the disaster. However, after studying all the factors of the case very carefully, and making special inquiry concerning the value that could be placed on the civil declarations of death that had been issued since the disaster, the Sacred Congregation came to the conclusion that no blanket permission to remarry

habere quiverunt: possuntne alias uxores accipere? R. Non posse ad alias nuptias transire, et detur Instructio anni 1792 de Prop. Fide, nempe '*Te non latere arbitror*'." S. C. S. Off., 12 feb. 1851—*Fontes,* n. 915. Cf. also the response of the Holy Office to the Vicar Apostolic of Transylvania, June 23, 1671, discussed at length, *supra* p. 31.

could be granted, nor could any special concessions from the general rules be permitted, and gave as its final decision that the Ordinaries were to settle particular cases of the proof of death arising from the disaster in accordance with the instruction of 1868.[23]

The caution manifested by the Holy See in connection with this disaster was required by several factors: (a) The short time that had elapsed since the disaster took place—a little over a year. (b) The disorganization that was still present at the scene of the disaster. (c) The fact that families were scattered far and wide. (d) The probability that when the excitement subsided, it would be possible in many cases to obtain testimonial evidence as to the death of the people still missing. (e) The obvious unreliability of the civil declarations of death in the circumstances just mentioned.

The question of presumption of death becomes of great importance in time of war; for despite the precautions taken by all modern military authorities, many soldiers fail to reappear after battle without definite proof of their death or capture being possible of attainment. When a soldier is missing in war he cannot for that reason be presumed dead if he fails to reappear in the course of time. According to the instruction of 1868 an investigation must be made of each case. It will be of value in such cases to get in touch with the immediate superior of the missing soldier, if this is possible, and find out what he knows about the man. Information should also be sought from the comrades of the missing soldier. Points concerning which inquiry should be made are: whether the missing soldier was engaged in a battle, whether he might have been captured by the enemy; was there any likelihood that he might have deserted; was he placed in a dangerous position?[24] There are three published decisions of the Holy See regarding the proof of death of missing soldiers.

A French soldier disappeared after the battle of St. Quentin, January 19, 1871, in the Franco-Prussian war. It was established

[23] S. C. de Sacr., 12 mart. 1910—*AAS*, II (1910), 196.

[24] S. C. S. Off., instr. 13 maii 1868, n. 7—*Fontes*, n. 1002.

that he took part in the battle and that nothing was ever heard of him thereafter. According to the testimony of his wife, he had made an agreement with seven of his comrades to meet at a certain place after the battle, and he alone failed to appear. A civil declaration of death was obtained in 1886. The Holy Office permitted remarriage to the wife, provided that the facts mentioned were established by authentic documents and trustworthy witnesses, and that it was further established that the man had affection for his wife and children, and that there was no reason for him to disappear.[25]

On March 1, 1896, an Italian army was overwhelmingly defeated by the Abyssinians at Adua (or Adowa). The Italians lost 4600 white and nearly 3000 native troops; the number of prisoners was estimated at between 2500 and 3500. The Holy Office, July 20, 1898, after consultation with the Holy Father, declared that the wives of soldiers missing in that battle could remarry, provided:

(a) It was certain that the men had taken part in the battle of Adua;

(b) That investigations had been made, as a result of which it was impossible to determine with certainty whether the man in question was alive or dead.

The Holy Office stated that this decision was given in consideration of the special circumstances of the case in question, and the existence of a valid presumption of death.[26]

This decision is noteworthy for several reasons: (1) It gave a

[25] "Dummodo ex authenticis documentis et ex testibus fide dignis saltem summarie et extraiudicialiter constet non solum de iis quae ab episcopo exponuntur, sed insuper Josephum N. sincero animo prosequutum fuisse uxorem et liberos, neque ullam adfuisse causam quare eos desereret, permitti posse Oratrici, ut Matrimonium ineat cum Ludovico N. . . . " S. C. S. Off., 17 apr. 1887—*AER,* VIII (1893), 144.

[26] "Dummodo agatur de viris, qui certo adstiterunt pugnae de Adua, et, peractis opportunis investigationibus, indubitanter dignosci nequeat an vir reapse mortuus ceciderit, attentis specialibus circumstantiis in casu exposito occurentibus, et valida praesumptione obitus, Ordinarius permittere poterit transitum ad alias nuptias." S. C. S. Off., 20 iul, 1898—*ASS,* XXXI (1898-1899), 252.

decision for a large group of persons; (2) its provisions on the face of it are mild compared with other decisions of the Holy See; (3) it permitted remarriage after the lapse of but two years from the time the men had become missing; (4) it was given as a guide in a later decision by the Sacred Congregation of the Sacraments in 1910.[27] Nevertheless is cannot be said that this decision is indicative of the adoption by the Holy See of a milder attitude towards the question of proof of death than that exhbited in earlier instructions and decisions.[28] It should be noted that the Holy Office required an adequate investigation in each individual case. Furthermore the Holy Office stated that there were special circumstances in the case leading to the decision.[29] Although the Sacred Congregation of the Sacraments (March 12, 1910) stated that among the circumstances which the Holy Office took into consideration in giving this decision were the illicit amours of the widows of the missing men, it indicates that there were others, possibly the ferocity with which the Abyssinians traditionally treated their prisoners.

The Sacred Congregation of the Sacraments decided in 1910 the case of a soldier who served in the Russian army in the Russo-Japanese war of 1904-1905. This soldier took part in the battle of Mukden, Manchuria, which lasted from Feb. 19 to March 10, 1905, when the city fell to the Japanese. The Russians lost 97,000 men in this battle. It was established with certainty from the military authorities that the soldier had taken part in the battle. The Sacred Congregation in arriving at its decision placed

[27] S. C. de Sacr., 16 dec. 1910—*Fontes,* n. 2104.

[28] "Eo enim in casu [Adua case] declaratio R. Pontificis non supplevit defectum certitudinis. Nam R. Pontifex sua declaratione non potest supplere, quod iure divino requiritur, atque nequit reddere certum, quod tantum est probabile. Hinc si revera permittit secundas nuptias, potius signum habetur veram adfuisse moralem certitudinem, quae dubium prudens excluserit." —Wernz, *Ius Decretalium,* IV, n. 370, nota 70.

[29] The Sacred Congregation of the Sacraments (12 mart. 1910—*AAS,* II [1910], 198) commenting on this decision says: "Ex quo apparet opportunas investigationes esse prius faciendas et quatenus hae evadunt sine effectu, perpendendae sunt speciales casus circumstantiae una simul cum valida mortis presumptione."

great stress on a document issued by the Russian military authorities in connection with the missing soldier. The Sacred Congregation permitted the wife to remarry, and stated that in any similar cases arising out of this war the decision of the Holy Office in the Adua case was to be applied.[30] It will be noted that a period of five years elapsed between the disappearance of the soldier and the declaration of the Holy See.

Taking into account the instruction of 1868 and the above mentioned decisions of the Sacred Congregations in cases of missing soldiers, the Ordinary would seem justified in declaring a missing soldier dead and permitting his wife to remarry when the following conditions are verified:

(1) When it is established that the soldier took part in a battle and was not seen again.

(2) If careful investigation in accordance with the instruction of 1868 fails to discover any trace of the missing man.

(3) If his married life was happy and there was no apparent reason for him to disappear.

(4) If a reasonable length of time, which will depend on various circumstances, has elapsed to give the missing person ample opportunity to get in touch with his family, in the event that he was captured by the enemy.[31] It may not be amiss to give here an example of the regulations issued by most of the German Bishops to the pastors at the beginning of the World War, with reference to the information which should be put in the Church

[30] S. C. de Sacr., 16 dec. 1910—*Fontes,* n. 2104.

[31] It would seem that an instruction issued by the Bishop of Trier, Germany, November 12, 1923 *(AKKR,* CIII [1923], 191) can hardly be said to be in harmony with the instructions and decisions of the Holy See. In this instruction to his clergy the Bishop of Trier stated that at that time when the disorder occasioned by the World War had subsided, there was need of regarding as still alive only such soldiers in the War who had not lived on peaceful terms with their wives. For this reason he decided that when the wife of a missing soldier wished to remarry, the pastor had to ascertain merely whether the first marriage was happy or not. If it was found to have been a happy one, the pastor could proceed without more ado; otherwise he should refer the case to the Diocesan Curia.

records concerning the death, etc., of members of their parishes serving in the War. Typical is the instruction of the Bishop of Osnabrück, issued Nov. 25, 1914:

> The death record can be a guide of the greatest importance for questions that arise later with regard to those participating in the war. For this reason we order the following for this diocese:
>
> 1. The names of those who die in battle or in hospitals, as a result of wounds or sickness, are to be entered in the death register. In addition there should be a book in the parish archives in which should be listed official and private news concerning the death, wounding, capture, or missing status of members of the parish; this information should be carefully gathered together and indexed. Especially should copies be made of all official notifications.
>
> 2. If the fact of death is certified by an official ecclesiastical, State or military bureau, the entry of death is to be made in the death register forthwith.
>
> The person keeping the Church books will in so far as is practical get in touch with the civil bureaus for matters of this kind.
>
> 3. The entry can also be made in the death register when the official list of casualties announces the death of the soldier, and his death is otherwise established (e.g., through the communication of an eye-witness). In the entry the number of the casualty list and other means of proof are to be indicated.
>
> 4. When the fact of death is doubtful, the entry should not be made in the death register. However, any trustworthy news which arrives later on concerning the soldier in question is to be carefully gathered and placed in the parish archives.
>
> 5. In all cases in which the wife of a soldier, who has failed to return from the front, wishes to contract a new marriage, and it is not possible to prove the death of the husband with certainty, the matter is to be reported immediately to the diocesan curia.[32]

Article II. Common Opinion

Common opinion *(fama)* [33] can be adduced as an argument to

[32] Hilling, "Kriegsverschollenheit und Eheschliessung"—*AKKR*, XCV (1915), 160-163.

[33] " . . . fama seu communis de viri morte opinio . . . " S. C. de Sacr., 25 iun. 1915—*Fontes*, n. 2112.

prove the death of a spouse, provided that it is supported by other evidence.[34] The instruction of 1868[35] follows the rules for the use of common opinion in proving death as laid down by Sanchez.[36] These are as follows:

(1) The existence of the common opionion concerning the death of the person in question must be proved by the testimony of two witnesses, who are absolutely trustworthy, and who have heard the opinion from reliable people.

(2) The common opinion must be based on some reasonable cause: for example, if a person boarded a ship which had to pass through an area that was heavily mined and which never arrived at its destination; or if he went into battle and never reappeared again, although diligent efforts were made to find him. Therefore, when witnesses testify to the existence of common opinion of a person's death, they must be examined closely as to the basis of this opinion.[37]

(3) The common opinion must be held by the greater part of the people of the district. In deciding whether this opinion is held by the greater number, only those people should be considered who are prudent and reliable members of the community. Thus, the witnesses who testify to the existence of public opinion must be able to give testimony to indicate that the opinion is held by a majority of the reliable people in the community.

[34] Sanchez, *De Sancto Matrimonii Sacramento,* lib. II, disp. 46, n. 15; Schmalzgrueber, lib. IV, tit. 21, n. 17.

[35] "Fama quoque aliis adiuta adminiculis argumentum de obitu constituit, hisce tamen conditionibus, nimirum: quod a duobus saltem testibus fide dignis et iuratis comprobetur, qui deponant de rationabili causa ipsius famae: an eam acceperint a maiori et saniori parte populi, et an ipsi de eadem fama recte sentiant; nec sit dubium illam fuisse concitatam ab illis in quorum commodum inquiritur." S. C. S. off., instr. 13 maii 1868, n. 8.

[36] *Op. cit.,* lib. 11, disp. 46, nn. 16-17. Cf. also Schmalzgrueber, lib. IV, tit. 21, n. 18.

[37] "Et ratio est, quia fama originem a probabilibus causis trahere debet: vox enim vana vulgi certo authore, et rationibus probabilibus carens, attendenda non est." —Sanchez, *De Sancto Matrimonii Sacramento,* lib. II, disp. 46, n. 16.

(4) The witnesses must themselves believe that the common opinion is correct.

(5) It must be established that the common opinion was not inspired by individuals who had an interest in proving the death of the missing spouse.[38]

Common opinion of the death of an absent husband or wife has been accepted as adminicular evidence in a number of cases decided by the Holy See.[39] In a case decided in 1900 the common opinion in the community that a man had died in the Cuban civil war of 1868-1878 was very influential in leading the Holy Office to grant a declaration of death of the missing spouse and permission to his wife to remarry.[40]

Article III. Presumption Cases

Before a reasonable presumption of death may be said to be established, it is necessary that the various conjectures, indications and circumstances, taken together give rise to moral certainty of the death of the spouse in question. The ultimate decision as to whether in a particular case they unite to cause moral certitude depends on the judge in the case, who in the administrative process is the Ordinary or his delegate.[41] The best guide in evaluating the factors in a case of presumed death will be the decisions of the Sacred Congregations in such cases. For this reason the recent decisions of the Sacred Congregations in cases of presumed death will be briefly summarized here, in order to show the evidence which led the Holy See to declare the missing persons dead in these cases.[42]

A man who had returned to Spain after many years in Cuba married a Spanish girl in 1862. Six months later he left her

[38] Payen *(De Matrimonio,* I, n. 406) notes that especially in China great care must be taken to see that this fifth condition is verified.

[39] S. C. de Sacr., 18 dec. 1914—*Fontes,* n. 2109; S. C. de Sacr., 25 iun. 1915—*Fontes,* n. 2112; S. C. de Sacr., 25 febr. 1916—*Fontes,* n. 2115; S. C. Sacr., 19 ian. 1917—*Fontes,* n. 2117; S. C. de Sacr., 18 nov. 1920—*AAS,* XIV (1922), 96.

[40] S. C. S. Off., 18 iul. 1900—*AER,* XXIV (1901), 387.

[41] S. C. S. Off., instr. 13 maii 1868, n. 6—*Fontes,* n. 1002.

[42] For some other presumed death cases cf. *supra,* pp. 89, 91-94.

on the pretext of business and returned to Cuba. For three years he kept up correspondence with his wife; his letters then ceased, and although his wife wrote many times to him after that, no answer was ever received. A public rumor (*rumor publicus*) based on reports of Spaniards returning from Cuba, circulated in the home district of the wife that her husband was engaged in the slave trade and was leading a very irregular and evil life. Seven years after the correspondence ceased, rumors began to spread that he had died in the Cuban civil war which was waged from 1868-1878. The woman made extensive investigations, especially among people she knew in Cuba, the re sult of which was that all stated her husband died in the rebellion, without mentioning any eye-witnesses, time or place of death. In 1874 the ecclesiastical authorities refused to permit remarriage; she then entered concubinage.

In a later process involving the same case two witnesses who had served as soldiers in the civil war and knew the missing husband testified that they had asked many people in Cuba about him, and all had stated that he died in the rebellion; these two witnesses had been unable to find any eye-witness of his death. Two relatives of the woman and the pastor testified to their belief in the man's death, also the woman herself. The pastor also testified to the existence of common opinion in the community that the man was dead. The vicar general stated that he had moral certitude of the man's death and gave his reasons: the advanced age of the man (76) if he were still living, in view of the kind of life he had led; the consistent reports of his death from Cuba over a period of twenty-eight years; the fact that his family had not heard of him, and believed him dead; the statements and opinion of everyone. The Holy Office permitted the wife to remarry.[43]

The Sacred Congregation of the Sacraments in 1909 permitted a wife to remarry whose husband had been missing for about twenty years. The missing husband, a man of fifty years of

[43] S. C. S. Off., 18 iul. 1900—*AER,* XXIV (1901), 387; *AKKR,* LXXXI (1901), 345.

age, had left Italy to work in Brazil. For the first year after he left he wrote to his wife every month; in the last letter received from him he stated that he intended to return home in the near future. Four months later a letter was received from a friend of his in Brazil stating that he had died. This person died himself during the same year. Both the letters of the missing spouse and the letter announcing his death were lost. However, the Sacred Congregation permitted the wife to remarry in consideration of the following circumstances: (a) The missing person would be 70 years of age, if he were still living, and his health was not good. (b) There was nothing to indicate that the friend who announced his death had any reason for lying. (c) The alleged deceased had the greatest affection for his wife and family, as evidenced by his regular correspondence during the first year of his absence; as a matter of fact he had indicated his intention of returning. (d) There was no apparent reason for him to disappear. (e) Nothing was ever heard of him by those who emigrated later on to the same district of Brazil. (f) It was the common opinion among those who knew him that he was dead.[44]

Another declaration of death was issued in 1909 by the Sacred Congregation of the Sacraments. A native of Newry, Ireland, had gone to Liverpool, England, to work as a sailor. He sent his wife money from time to time, and returned home to visit her whenever the occasion offered. After a year had elapsed without anything being heard from him, a letter arrived, the author of whom was unknown to the wife, announcing his death. He was mourned as dead by his relatives and friends. Ten years later the wife married a non-Catholic before a Protestant minister. The Sacred Congregation decided that the death of the missing person was established with moral certainty in the above mentioned circumstances, especially since the domestic life of the alleged deceased and his wife had been happy, and since nothing had been heard from him for over twenty years. The principal witnesses whose testimony was taken by the Bishop of Dromore were the

[44] S. C. de Sacr., 22 ian. 1909—*Il Monitore Ecclesiastico,* 3rd Series, I (1909), 200.

wife; her sister who testified to the arrival of the letter announcing the husband's death; and a friend of the missing man who had made several unsuccessful efforts to find out what had happened to him. Since the *Tametsi* was not published in Ireland, and the second marriage took place before the *Ne Temere* of 1908, it was considered valid, but the Bishop was instructed to see that the wife did suitable penance for marrying outside the Church, and that the usual precautions in connection with mixed marriages were taken.[45]

The Sacred Congregation of the Sacraments in 1914 permitted a wife to remarry whose husband had been missing for a long time. The circumstances leading to the presumption of death were as follows: (a) Many thorough investigations; (b) The long absence of the man (46 years) without any news despite thorough investigation, together with his advanced age (over 70) if he were still living, especially in view of his depraved morals. (c) The testimony of the son, that he was long ago told by two eye-witnesses (no longer available) that his father was dead, one of whom stated that his father went out in a boat to swim, that he did not reappear, and that his clothes were found on the bridge where he had left them.[46]

A decision of the Sacred Congregation of the Sacraments in 1915 is notable for two reasons: (a) All the presumptive evidence was negative and there was nothing positive to indicate the death of the missing spouse. (b) It is the only published decision of the Holy See in which the missing person was a woman. The facts which led to the establishment of the presumption of death were: (1) The missing woman would be about 72 years of age, if she were still alive; it was extremely unlikely that she would live to such an age, because of her addiction to liquor and her notorious immorality. She was very poor and made her living by being a servant, an avocation she could no longer follow due to her alcoholism. (2) Frequent investigations as to her where-

[45] S. C. de Sacr., 26 mart. 1909—*Il Monitore Ecclesiastico,* 3rd Series, I (1909), 201.

[46] S. C. de Sacr., 28 nov. 1914—*Fontes,* n. 2109.

abouts had been made both by the civil authorities and by her parents, and no trace of her was found. In the decision it is pointed out that in large cities such as the one where this woman lived, it is quite common for bodies to be buried without the names of the persons being known. Another factor in the decision, which permitted the husband to remarry, was the statement of the diocesan authorities that to them the death of the woman seemed very highly probable (*maxima probabilitas*). The time elapsed between the disappearance and the final decision was 38 years.[47]

In 1915 the Sacred Congregation of the Sacraments again gave a declaration of death in a case in which the presumption of the death of the missing spouse was based entirely on evidence of a negative character. A man left his homeland for America in order to escape a jail sentence for theft. For five years he corresponded with his wife. In his last letter he expressed his intention of soon returning home. From that time, 1894, no more was ever heard of him. A civil declaration of death was issued in 1906. In 1912 both the diocesan and the metropolitan Curiae decided *"non constare de morte Titii."* The latter Curia suggested sending the case to the Holy See. The reasons which led the Sacred Congregation to declare the missing spouse dead were as follows: (a) Exceptionally thorough investigations were made in the city in America where he had lived, without any trace of him being found. Notices were placed in language newspapers read in America by the people of his nationality. (b) The time limit of being cited to court and punished for his crime had elapsed before 1894. (c) The poor health of the man received weighty consideration from the Congregation. (d) The Sacred Congregation placed the greatest weight on the sudden and inexplicable cessation of correspondence in 1894, especially since his love for wife and family were so evident. The fact that in his last letter he said that he would return home soon was also

[47] S. C. de Sacr., 29 apr. 1915—*Fontes,* n. 2111.

considered very important. The time elapsed between the last letter and the decision of the Holy See was 21 years.[48]

In the year 1890 a man disappeared while on a journey from his place of work to visit relatives in another place. It was a dangerous journey in the course of which it was necessary to cross a large lake. The man in question was fond of liquor and had a bad arm. It was established that he was devoted to his wife and family. He had written to his wife, who at the time of his disappearance was visiting her parents, telling her of his intended trip. As further evidence that he did not intend to disappear it was brought out that, although only a poor man, he had taken nothing of value with him. Extensive investigation by his wife and by the mining company by which he was employed failed to find any trace of him. Nothing had been heard of him since his disappearance. It was the common opinion in the place where he worked that he died as the result of some accident. The Ordinary gave testimonials to the honesty and veracity of the woman, and gave his opinion in favor of the presumed death of the man. A period of over 25 years had elapsed between the time of disappearance and the decision of the Congregation.[49]

Another declaration of death of a missing person was issued by the Sacred Congregation of the Sacraments in 1917. In this case a man addicted to a dissolute life deserted his wife. In 1895 he joined the army and went to fight in Cuba. The following year he wrote to his relatives stating that he was in the hospital suffering from a serious pulmonary disease. He mentioned in his letter that deadly yellow fever was sweeping the country. He expressed his sorrow for his evil ways, and promised to return to his home and to his wife. No more was ever heard of him. From other sources the prevalence of yellow fever in Cuba at the time mentioned by the missing person was established. Although repeated investigations were made by his relatives, by the civil, military and ecclesiastical authorities, no trace of him was ever found. The rumor circulated that he died of the pestilence

[48] S. C. de Sacr., 25 iun. 1915—*Fontes,* n. 2112.

[49] S. C. de Sacr., 25 febr. 1916—*Fontes,* n. 2115.

in July, 1896. The fact that nothing was ever heard of him indicated that he either perished of the fever or fell in battle. The Congregation placed great emphasis on the long period of 21 years which had elapsed without any news having been heard of him.[50]

There is only one published decision issued since the Code by the Sacred Congregation of the Sacraments in a presumed death case, and this is a favorable one. It refers to a Spaniard who towards the end of 1902 or at the beginning of 1903 went to South America to work. He was devoted to his wife and family; he wrote to his wife and sent her money from time to time. One of his letters written in 1905 was produced and its contents indicate his good dispositions to his wife. He was a man of good character and faithful to his religious duties. A witness with whom he had been staying while abroad testified that towards the end of 1905 he left the city of Rosario de Santa Fè in the Argentine to go to a distant place to cut timber, and that nothing was ever heard of him thereafter. Extensive investigations were made but no trace of him was ever found. The parents of his wife even took a trip to South America to look for him but in vain. People returning from South America were questioned about him; the Spanish consul in Rosario de Santa Fè made investigations but could find nothing. It was alleged that the mother of the missing man had received word from America which led her to believe that he was dead. However, according to the pastor of the place, she refused to testify because she did not wish her son's wife to remarry. Witnesses testified to the common opinion *(fama)* of the people of the home district of the missing spouse that he was dead. A period of fifteen years had elapsed between the disappearance of the individual and the decision of the Sacred Congregation.[51]

A case was presented to the Rota from the Diocese of Valleyfield, Canada in 1928 on two scores: the nullity of the marriage was sought on the ground of previous bond *(ligamen)*, and an

[50] S. C. de Sacr., 19 ian. 1917—*Fontes,* n. 2117.

[51] S. C. de Sacr., 18 nov. 1920—*AAS,* XIV (1922), 96.

attempt was made to prove the death of the husband since he had been missing for many years. Extensive investigations had been made through the press, the police, and by the diocesan authorities, but no trace of him was found. His two brothers testified that they had heard nothing from him or about him since his mother's death in 1907. Evidence against the fact of death was the testimony of a witness who claimed that he had seen the man in question a few years before. The Rota stated (in discussing the "motiva in facto") that the evidence presented was not sufficient to give rise to moral certitude of the death of the missing person.[52]

[52] S. R. R., 19 oct. 1928, dec. XLIX—*Decisiones,* XX (1928), 426. Cf. also S. R. R., 27 iul. 1929, dec. XL—*Decisiones,* XXI (1929), 339.

Chapter VII

THE DECLARATION OF DEATH AND ITS LEGAL CONSEQUENCES

Article I. Decision and Recourse

A. *Moral Certitude*

Certitude is required before a declaration of death may be issued for the purpose of remarriage.[1] Mere probability will not suffice, and on the other hand metaphysical and physical certitude are not demanded.[2] What is required and suffices is moral certitude.[3] Certitude may be defined as "the fixed or firm assent or adherence of the mind to a truth, without any prudent fear of error."[4] Moral certitude is present when a thing is so certain, based on such strong grounds, that no reasonable doubt prevails against it. The instruction of 1868 (n. 6) identifies the two terms *maxima probabilitas* and *certitudo moralis*. The death of a former spouse will, then, be considered established when there is "such a weight of cumulative evidence of various kinds as will warrant that very high degree of probability which is commonly called 'practical' or 'moral' certitude."[5]

The necessity of moral certitude in questions of this type is evident for several reasons: a) in order that the unity and indissolubiliy of marriage be adequately safe-guarded; b) to avoid

[1] Canon 1069, § 2.

[2] A *defensor vinculi* was rebuked in a decision of the Sacred Congregation of the Council for insisting on metaphysical rather than moral certitude: "cum ipse [defensor vinculi], Sacros Canones et Instructionem Sacrae et Universalis Inquisitionis interpretans, tam anxius esset de certìtudine omnem penitus oppositi possibilitatem excludente, ut oblivisci videretur, in hoc genere quaestionum non certe metaphysicam, sed moralem certitudinem requiri." S. C. C., *in Mediolanen. Matrimonii,* 22 sept. 1860—Pallottini, "Matrimonium," § 14, nn. 36-41, 58-64.

[3] S. C. S. Off., 13 maii 1868—*Fontes,* n. 1002. Cf. Sanchez, *De Sancto Matrimonii Sacramento,* lib. II, disp. 46, n. 6.

[4] Coffey, *The Science of Logic* (New York: Peter Smith, 1938), II, 211.

[5] Coffey, *op. cit.,* II, 217.

the danger of contracting an invalid and adulterous union; c) because a person is presumed to be alive, until his death has been proved; and d) because if the death of a spouse is doubtful, "*melior est conditio prioris matrimonii possidentis.*"[6]

The ultimate determination of the existence of moral certitude in a particular case must be left to the prudent judgment of the person having the right to render a decision, and his judgment should be formed only after all circumstances bearing on the establishment of the death of the individual in question have been taken into account.[7]

B. *The Decision*

When the evidence has been presented and has been carefully evaluated by the Ordinary, several courses are open to him.

(a) If, despite the fact that as thorough an investigation has been made as is possible under the circumstances, the Ordinary is convinced that the death of the missing person is still open to grave doubts, he must declare that the death of the missing person has not been established with moral certitude and the petitioning party may not remarry.

(b) If, although moral certitude has not been established, the Ordinary feels that additional investigation might unearth evidence sufficiently strong to prove the death of the person in question, he may postpone a definite decision until a fuller investigation has been completed.

(c) If the investigation has been thoroughly made, and while the evidence is strong, it is not sufficiently conclusive to make the Ordinary morally certain of the death of the missing spouse, he should forward the case to the Sacred Congregation of the Sacraments.

(d) If the Ordinary is convinced that the death of the missing individual has been proved with moral certitude by the evidence presented, he should declare that the death of the absent

[6] Sanchez, *De Sancto Matrimonii Sacramento,* lib. II, disp. 46, n. 1.

[7] Sanchez, *op. cit.,* lib. II, disp. 46, n. 7. Cf. S. C. S. Off., 13 maii 1868, n. 6; canon 1869, § 3.

spouse has been established and give permission to the surviving spouse to remarry.

In all cases the petitioning party should be informed of the Ordinary's decision. Although not required by the instruction of 1868, it would seem fitting that, when a declaration of death has been issued, the Ordinary should see that this fact is noted in the death register of the parish to which the deceased formerly belonged. It would be prudent also to have the declaration noted in the marriage register of the Church where the first marriage took place.

The significance of the ecclesiastical declaration of death should be kept in mind by the Ordinary, and should be explained to the parties in favor of whom it is issued. Reduced to its true sense the ecclesiastical declaration of death signifies no more than this: The evaluation of all the circumstances and evidence in the case leads to the conclusion that the death of the missing partner is in so high a degree certain, and it is so beyond the sphere of probability that this person is still alive, that the surviving party cannot be required to feel himself bound any longer by the impediment of *ligamen,* and because of the purely theoretical though possible return of the missing person to forego marriage for the duration of life. In consequence of this the Church no longer feels herself justified in preventing a remarriage on the part of the surviving party, and therefore gives him permission to remarry.

C. *Recourse*

It is the wish of the Holy See that, when cases of proof of death arise, the Ordinary should endeavor to settle the case himself. Only when, after a thorough investigation and after making use of the process of the instruction of 1868, he cannot reach moral certainty as to the fact of death, should he forward the case to Rome.[8] When the case is sent to Rome, the acts of the case them-

[8] S. C. S. Off., 13 maii 1868—*Fontes,* n. 1002; S. C. de Sacr., 18 nov. 1920—*AAS,* XIV (1922), 96. The published decisions of the Holy See reveal more than one case which could have been settled by the Ordinary himself without recourse to Rome. For example, the Vicar General of the diocese of Zamora sent a case to the Holy See, although he had moral

selves or an accurate transcription should be forwarded along with the recourse.[9] Since 1908 the Sacred Congregation of the Sacraments is the competent congregation for cases of this kind.

If the Ordinary rejects a petition for declaration of death of a husband or wife, the interested parties have the right of recourse to the Sacred Congregation of the Sacraments.[10]

Whenever recourse is to be made, it must be made directly to the Congregation of the Sacraments. Under the present discipline the Metropolitan and the Rota are not competent to accept cases of this kind handled in administrative procedure.[11]

Article II. The Impediment of Crime

In very many cases, when the Ordinary issues a declaration of death of a first spouse, it will be necessary to grant a dispensation from the impediment of crime.

certainty of the person's death. S. C. S. Off., 18 iul. 1900—*AER*, XXIV (1901), 387. In another case sent to the Holy See there were one eyewitness, four hearsay witnesses, and very strong adminicular testimony as to the death of the spouse in question. S. C. de Sacr., 18 dec. 1914—*Fontes*, n. 2109.

[9] "Quod si non obstantibus regulis hucusque notatis, res adhuc incerta et implexa illis videatur, ad S. Sedem recurrere debebunt, actis omnibus cum ipso recursu transmissis, aut saltem diligenter expositis."—S. C. S. Off., instr. 13 maii 1868, n. 11. "Ordinarius canonicas inquisitiones complere velit ad normam instructionis S. C. S. Officii a. 1868, *Matrimonii Vinculo*. Si peractis enunciatis inquisitionibus, iudicium sibi efformare non valeat, quo transitus ad alias nuptias permittere queat, tunc omnia acta ad hanc S. Congregationem mittat." S. C. de Sacr., 18 nov. 1920—*AAS*, XIV (1922), 96.

[10] S. C. S. Off., 8 maii 1891—*Fontes*, n. 1135. The Holy See granted a declaration of death in a case where both the diocesan and the metropolitan Curiae had given negative decisions. S. C. de Sacr., 25 iun. 1915—*Fontes*, n. 2112.

[11] Canon 1601; Pontificia Commissio ad Codicis Canones Authentice Interpretandos, 22 maii 1923—*AAS*, XVI (1924), 215; cf. *supra*, p. 49. Several authors (Kaas, *Kriegsverschollenheit und Wiederverheiratung*, p. 115; Lanier, *Procédure Matrimoniale*, p. 9; Triebs, *Handbuch des kanonischen Eherechts*, p. 312) have mistakenly stated that in cases ot this kind, tried in administrative procedure, recourse could be made to the Metropolitan.

The impediment of crime can be incurred in several different ways (cf. canon 1075). To mention the most frequent type, it is incurred by parties who, during the legitimate marriage of one of them commit adultery, and make a mutual promise of marriage with each other, or attempt marriage at least civilly,[12] When marriage is attempted adultery will always be presumed in the external forum.[13] If the parties contract or attempt marriage in bad faith, when there is doubt as to the death of an absent spouse of one of them, the impediment of crime will be presumed, and the parties are restrained by the presumed impediment until it is proved that the spouse was dead at the time of the attempted marriage. For the presumption here is that everyone is presumed to be among the living until his death is proved.[14] Therefore, whenever a couple have been living together or have attempted marriage before a declaration of death of a former spouse is issued, a dispensation from the impediment of crime will be in order. In other cases it may be will to grant the dispensation *ad cautelam.*

When the Holy See grants permission for remarriage because of the presumed death of a spouse, a dispensation from the impediment of crime is always implicitly included in the permission.[15] However, this dispensation is not included when the Ordinary grants a declaration of death in such a case, and the Ordinary must always explicitly grant a dispensation from the impediment of crime, when it seems necessary.[16]

[12] Canon 1075, n. 1.

[13] Cappello, *De Matrimonio,* n. 404.

[14] Cappello, *De Matrimonio,* nn. 404, 481; Gasparri, *De Matrimonio,* I, n. 673; Donohue, *The Impediment of Crime* (The Catholic University of America, Canon Law Studies, n. 69, Washington: The Catholic University of America, 1931), p. 42; Wanenmacher, *Canonical Evidence in Marriage Cases,* n. 491.

[15] Canon 1053. The dispensation is included only for the impediment of crime as described in canon 1075, n. 1, not for the species of the impediment enumerated in canon 1075, nn. 2 and 3.

[16] The Ordinary may grant the dispensation if he has the power from his Quinquennial Faculties or from an indult; otherwise it must be obtained from the Holy See.

ARTICLE III. THE LEGAL CONSEQUENCES OF ERRONEOUS DECLARATION OF DEATH AND THE SOLUTION OF DOUBTFUL CASES

A. *Return of a Spouse Thought Dead*

The legal nature of the ecclesiastical declaration of death is purely declarative, not constitutive. The validity of a subsequent marriage is not affected by the declaration; the second marriage will be valid or invalid, depending on whether the first spouse was dead or alive at the time the second marriage took place. For this reason, if the decision proves erroneous, and the missing person actually returns, it is the first marriage which is valid, and the second is invalid. In this case the parties of the second marriage may not live together as man and wife, and the first marriage should be reinstated.[17] The reinstatement of the first marriage may not always prove feasible, but the separation of the parties to the second marriage must always be insisted upon.

In an exceptional case the first marriage may not have been consummated. In such an eventuality, there is the possibility of obtaining a dispensation from the Holy See for a marriage ratified but not consummated *(dispensatio super matrimonio rato et non consummato)*.[18] If the returning spouse is an infidel (unbaptized), the Pauline privilege or the *privilegium fidei* may possibly be used. Outside of these exceptional cases, when a former spouse thought dead is proved to be living, the parties to the second marriage must separate.

If the parties to a second marriage refuse to separate after it has been proved with certainty that the former spouse of one of them is still living, they incur the impediment of crime.[19] Furthermore they will be considered as bigamists, and become liable

[17] Lucius III—c. 2, X, *de secundis nuptiis,* IV, 21; S. Leo I—c. 1, C. XXXIV, q. 1 and 2; S. C. de Prop. Fide, instr. a. 1792—*Fontes,* n. 4632.

[18] In time of war, it sometimes happens that couples are married immediately before the husband leaves for the front. It may be possible to prove non-consummation in some of these cases.

[19] Canon 1075, n. 1. Cf. *supra,* p. 110.

to the penalties leveled by the Code against bigamists.[20] They will icur infamy *ipso facto* (from which they can be relieved only by a dispensation from the Holy See);[21] as a result they are deprived of the right to perform legitimate ecclesiastical acts.[22] If they persist in their illicit union, and disregard the warning of the Ordinary, they become liable to the penalties of excommunication and personal interdict *ferendae sententiae*.[23] As public sinners, they are excluded from membership in pious associations,[24] they are to be excluded from the reception of the Eucharist,[25] they are irregular *ex delicto*,[26] and are to be deprived of Christian burial unless they show signs of penitence before death.[27]

When it is certainly proved that the first spouse of one of the parties was alive at the time of the second marriage, the second marriage will be considered in canon law as a putative marriage, provided that at least one of the parties was in good faith at the time of the marriage. Such a marriage will be considered putative until both parties become certain of the nullity of the marriage.[28] All children born or conceived of such marriage are legitimate.[29] However, it is necessary that the good faith, on the part of at least one party to the putative marriage, be present both at the time of the marriage contract and at the time of conception.[30]

The case may arise in which the missing person is proved to have been alive at the time of the second marriage, but died sub-

[20] Canon 2356.

[21] Canon 2295.

[22] Canons 2294, § 1, 2256, § 2.

[23] Canon 2356.

[24] Canon 693, § 1.

[25] Canon 855, § 1.

[26] Canon 985, n. 3.

[27] Canon 1240, § 1.

[28] Canon 1015, § 4. For a marriage to be considered putative, it must have been celebrated *in facie ecclesiae*.—Cappello, *De Matrimonio*, n. 48.

[29] Canon 1114. As legitimate will be presumed children born within six months after the celebration of such a marriage, and within ten months after it ceases.—Canon 1115, § 2.

[30] Cappello, *De Matrimonio*, n. 746.

sequently. Two possibilities are open to the parties of the second marriage:

(a) They may separate, and if they obtain a declaration of nullity from the competent eccesiastical tribunal, they will both be free to enter other marriages. It should be noted in this case, that if one of the parties entered the marriage in good faith, and the other in bad faith, the former is perfectly free to separate from his partner, but the latter is bound in justice to have the marriage convalidated, if the person in good faith so desires; grave misconduct on the part of the person in good faith would of course free the person in bad faith from his obligation.[31]

(b) The marriage may be convalidated. Radical sanation *(sanatio in radice)* of the marriage is out of the question, since *(ligamen)* is an impediment of the divine law, and the Church, does not grant a radical sanation for a marriage contracted with an impediment of the natural or divine law, not even from the moment when the impediment ceased.[32] Furthermore, the cessation of the impediment is not enough to convalidate the marriage. The consent must be renewed.[33] Since the impediment of *ligamen* is public by nature and practically always in fact,[34] the renewal of the consent must take place before the pastor and two witnesses.[35]

[31] Chelodi, *Ius Matrimoniale,* n. 77; Payen, *De Matrimonio,* I, n. 1053; Kaas, *Kriegsverschollenheit und Wiederverheiratung,* p. 117.

[32] Canon 1139, § 2.

[33] Canons 1133, 1134.

[34] An impediment is public when it can be proved in the external forum.—Canon 1037.

[35] Canon 1135, § 1. "Only when the impediment which invalidated the marriage is occult both in nature and in fact can the prescriptions of the canon [canon 1135, § 2 and §3] be applied."—Brennan, *The Simple Convalidation of Marriage* (The Catholic University of America, Canon Law Studies, n. 102, Washington: The Catholic University of America, 1937), p. 56. About the only time when the impediment would be secret, would be if the first marriage took place according to canon 1098 and cannot be proved in the external forum. It is a probable opinion, according to Payen (*De Matrimonio,* I, n. 1067), that in such a case if only one of the parties was conscious of the impediment and there is grave difficulty connected with informing the other, the consent can be renewed by the party conscious of the impediment privately and secretly.

If the parties are considered as validly married in the district where they live and the fact of the impediment is there unknown, a marrage of conscience is possible, in which the pastor and the witnesses would be bound to secrecy.[36]

If the parties to the second marriage had married in bad faith, i.e., while doubtful of the death of the first spouse, the impediment of crime (canon 1075) is incurred.[37] For this reason, before the convalidation of the second marriage takes place, a dispensation from the impediment of crime should be obtained.[38]

B. *Nullity Cases*

If the nullity of a marriage is alleged on the ground that a previous marriage of one of the parties was in existence at the time the second marriage was contracted, the question of the nullity of the second marriage will have to be settled by an ecclesiastical tribunal. Before the tribunal declares the second marriage null, it must be proved with certainty that the first spouse was living at the time of the second marriage;[39] it must be established that the first marriage was a valid marriage,[40] and if the first spouse had died since the second marriage was contracted, it must be proved that the second marriage had not been convalidated.

If the fact of the previous marriage is evident from an authentic document, the informal documentary process of canon 1990 may be used. However, if a document is not available, and an investigation of the fact of death in accordance with the instruction of 1868 is required, the case seems beyond the scope of the process of canon 1990 and should be handled by the regular process.[41]

If the parties to the second marriage were both unbaptized,

[36] Canon 1104.

[37] Cappello, *De Matrimonio,* n. 481; Gasparri, *De Matrimonio,* I, n. 673; Donohue, *The Impediment of Crime,* p. 42.

[38] Cf. *supra,* p. 110.

[39] S. C. S. Off., 22 mart. 1865, ad I—*Fontes,* n. 982; S. C. S. Off., 21 nov. 1866—*Fontes,* n. 997; S. C. de Prop. Fide, instr. a. 1883—*Fontes,* n. 4901; S. R. R., 27 iul. 1929, dec. XL—*Decisiones,* XXI (1929), 339.

[40] Manning, *Presumptions of Law in Marriage Cases,* pp. 61-65.

[41] Kennedy, *The Special Matrimonial Process in Cases of Evident Nullity,* p. 120.

then according to the *natural law* renewal of consent is not required, in the event that the first spouse died after the second marriage was contracted, and it is sufficient for convalidation that the consent exchanged by the parties on the occasion of the first ceremony still perseveres.[42] Therefore, when two unbaptized persons are involved, the marriage may not be declared null, unless it is certain that the first spouse was alive during the whole period that the marital consent in the second union continued.

Since most canonists hold that the State has the right to enact matrimonial legislation (including the constitution of impediments) for marrages of unbaptized non-Catholics,[43] in a case of this kind the judge should take into account the State legislation both with regard to common law marriage[44] and the convalidation of marriage.[45]

C. *Doubtful Cases*

Another possibility is the case in which after a second marriage has taken place doubt arises as to whether the first spouse of one of the parties is really dead or not. According to all authors no attention is paid to a slight doubt, at least after investigation has been made.[46] The question becomes one of considerable difficulty when a grave and prudent doubt arises as to the death of the first spouse. The consequences in the external forum will be discussed first, then those that follow in the internal forum.

The External Forum

There are three possibilities in such marriages. Both parties may have entered the marriage in good faith; one of the parties may have entered the marriage in good faith, the other in bad faith; both parties may have entered the marriage in bad faith.

A marriage of this kind would have been entered in good faith

[42] Gasparri, *De Matrimonio,* II, n. 1193; Brennan, *The Simple Convalidation of Marriage,* p. 41.

[43] Cf. Cappello, *De Matrimonio,* nn. 75-80.

[44] Cf. Doheny, *Canonical Procedure in Matrimonial Cases,* p. 435.

[45] Cf. *infra,* p. .27

[46] C. 44, X, *de sententia excommunicationis,* V, 39. Cf. Gasparri, *De Matrimonio,* I, n. 564.

when the parties were convinced that they were free to marry. It would take place especially when the parties have previously obtained an ecclesiastical declaration of the death of the first spouse. Even though a legitimate ecclesiastical declaration was not obtained, it would still be possible for the parties to remain in good faith.[47] This could happen if the parties, either being morally certain themselves that the first spouse was dead, or not realizing that moral certainty of the first spouse's death was necessary, presented themselves to a careless or ignorant pastor who failed to turn the case over to the Ordinary for settlement.

Bad faith here means contracting a second marriage with a substantial doubt concerning the dissolution of the the first marriage. In bad faith would be those parties who, although warned that there was not sufficient evidence to indicate that the first marriage had been dissolved by death, either forged a certificate of death, or concealed the fact of the first marriage when they approached a priest for the second marriage.[48]

When both parties are in good faith, and a third party discovers that there is doubt as to the dissolution of the first marriage, they are to be left in good faith.[49] If one or both of the parties themselves should discover the doubt, an investigation must be made. If after the investigation the doubt still remains, the parties may continue to live together as man and wife.[50] The same is to be

[47] Lehmkuhl, *Theologia Moralis* (11. ed., Friburgi Brisgoviae, 1910), II, n. 1077.

[48] Payen, *De Matrimonio,* I, n. 1054.

[49] "Quamobrem, si qui iam nova coniugia contraxerunt, et quidem in bona fide, existimantes se per interitum coniugis a priori coniugii vinculo absolutos, relinquendi sunt in bona fide, quia bonae fidei possessor turbari a possessione non debet." S. C. de Prop. Fide, instr. a 1792--*Fontes,* n. 4632.

"Caecilia, marito a rebellibus capto, nec post tres annos amplius comparente, eum habuit pro mortuo, et, absente proprio sacerdote, nupsit Petro rei conscio, sed similiter de morte prioris viri persuaso. Missionarius, cum impossibile sit scire vel inquirere utrum Paulus vir prior vivat, censet eos non esse inquietandos, et relinquendos esse in matrimonio donec non habeatur certus nuntius de vita Pauli. An bene? R. Relinquendos esse in bona fide." S. C. S. Off., 22 mart. 1865—Fontes, n. 982.

[50] Schmalzgrueber, lib. IV, tit. 21, n. 26. It is understood, of course,

said when only one of the parties entered the marriage in good faith.[51] When the parties entered the marriage in bad faith, that is, with a positive and prudent doubt concerning the death of the first spouse, they cannot be considered as possessors in good faith, and must be separated. In the external forum the right of the first spouse prevails against the rights of the spouses of the second marriage in this case.[52]

If the parties refuse to separate, they are to be treated as public sinners, and are to be denied the sacraments.[53]

A very important point must be noted in regard to this last case. Not only is it illicit for these people to live together, but the one who is otherwise free to marry, may not marry anyone else until it is proved that the missing spouse of the first marriage was certainly alive at the time of the second marriage.[54] The reason is that, since it is doubtful whether the first marriage is dissolved, it is also doubtful whether the second marriage is valid or not, and in view of the probable validity of the second marriage a further marriage is forbidden.[55]

that, after the investigation has been completed, the death of the first spouse is still solidly probable.

[51] S. C. de Prop. Fide, instr. a. 1792—*Fontes,* n. 4632. Cf. Payen, *De Matrimonio,* I, n. 1056.

[52] "Sponsos tamen non posse admitti ad Sacramentorum participationem, nisi praevia eorundem separatione." S. C. S. Off., 28 iun. 1865—*Fontes,* n. 984. "Si demum uterque mala fide contraxit, iam sunt omnino separandi." S. C. de Prop. Fide, instr. a. 1792—*Fontes,* n. 4632. Cf. also S. C. S. Off., 22 mart. 1865; S. C. S. Off., 21 nov. 1866—*Fontes,* nn. 982, 997.

[53] Cf. *supra,* p. 111. Payen (*De Matrimonio,* I, n. 1060) would make an exception to this strict ruling under certain circumstances, permitting the parties to live together and to receive the sacraments, namely when they had lived together for many years, and the danger of scandal was removed.

[54] Cf. *supra,* p. 114, note 39.

[55] "Titio capto a rebellibus, eoque frustra per duos aut tres annos desiderato, Martha eius uxor sine assistentia proprii sacerdotis, quae ad valorem ibi necessaria non est, et contra monitum missionariorum, contraxit cum Marco. Marcus autem graviter reprehensus a missionariis, vult quidem dimittere Martham, sed petit ad alias transire nuptias. Quid

The Internal Forum

When two people marry in good faith, and a doubt arises after the marriage concerning the death of the former spouse of one of them, an investigation must be made. Before the investigation is made, if one is aware of the doubt and the other is not, the one doubting may not request the *debitum* but may grant it upon the other's request.[56] If both parties are in doubt as to the death of the first spouse in question, they must suspend marriage relations until the investigation has been completed.[57] If, on the completion of the investigation into the death of the former spouse, the doubt is still not settled according to the great majority of authors the parties may resume normal marriage relations; both have the right to ask for the *debitum*. Those who favor this view apply to the use of marriage the general rules governing possession in good faith.[58]

agendum? R. Separandos esse coniuges, et virum non posse secundas inire nuptias, usque dum moraliter sit certum, quo tempore ipse matrimonium iniit cum muliere de qua agitur, primum virum eiusdem mulieris non obiisse." S. C. S. Off., 22 mart. 1865—*Fontes,* n. 982.

"Et relate ad primum casum, quum neophyta et secundus vir eius sint ambo in mala fide, separandos esse, et monendum etiam virum non posse ad alias transire nuptias, nisi constito virum absentem adhuc vixisse quando secundum matrimonium tentatum fuit." S. C. S. Off., 21 nov. 1866—*Fontes,* n. 997. Cf. S. R. R., 27 iul. 1929, rec. XL—*Decisiones,* XXI (1929), 339; canons 1014, 1019, 1069, § 2.

[56] C. 44, X, *de sententia excommunicationis,* V, 39; St. Alphonsus De Ligorio, *Theologia Moralis* (Augustae Taurinorum, 1891), lib. VI, n. 903.

[57] Sanchez, *De Sancto Matrimonii Sacramento,* lib. II, disp. 41, n. 55; Schmalzgrueber, lib. IV, tit. 21, n. 27.

[58] "Ratio . . . quia in dubio melior est conditio possidentis; et ipsa possessio bonae fidei rei sic possessae liberum usum tribuit."—Schmalzgrueber, lib. IV, tit. 21, n. 28. " . . . quod, si post diligentem inquisitionem solum maneat dubium, uterque reddere et petere possit, probatur ex illa universali Doctrina, quod, si bonae fidei possessor incipiat dubitare, rem esse alienam, et post diligentem inquisitionem dubium vincere nequeat, possit rem non tantum retinere, sed ea etiam uti, prout probat Sanchez . . . , et ergo idem erit de possessione et usu Matrimonii."—Reiffenstuel, lib. IV, tit. 21, n. 28. Among the other authors favoring this opinion may be mentioned Sanchez, *De Sancto Matrimonii Sacramento,* lib. II, disp. 41, n. 55; Lehmkuhl, *Theologia Moralis,* II, n. 1076;

For the case in which both parties entered the marriage in bad faith authors are not agreed. Before an investigation is made, it is clear that neither party has any right either to request or to grant the *debitum.* After an investigation has been made, and the doubt remains unsolved, it is a probable opinion that the parties may both request and grant the *debitum.*[59] However, the contrary opinion seems intrinsically much more probable in the light of the general norms with regard to possessors in bad faith.[60]

Noldin, *De Sexto Praecepto et De Usus Matrimonii* (30 ed., Oeniponte: Fel Rauch, 1938), n. 98; Genicot-Salsmans, *Institutiones Theologiae Moralis,* II, n. 445. St. Alphonsus (*Theologia Moralis,* lib. VI, n. 906) holds the contrary view: "At hoc minime admittendum, nam in dubio de morte prioris coniugis, sive nuptiae sint initae cum bona fide sive cum dubia fide, nunquam coniux dubitans petere poterit, nisi de morte prioris coniugis habeatur certitudo, aut saltem tanta praesumptio quae moralem certitudinem statuat. Alias, si tantum probabilitas de morte habeatur, nequit unquam coniux ille dubitans petere, tum quia tunc remanet probabile periculum iniuriae prioris coniugis, iuxta dicta in tractatu de conscientia quem ipse condidi [lib. I, nn. 42, 52], tum quia eo casu possidet prius matrimonium, donec constet fuisse solutum." Cf. also St. Alphonsus, *op. cit.,* n. 900. Gasparri (*De Matrimonio,* I, n. 564) holds the same view: " . . . ideoque si uterque serio dubitat, neuter petere ac reddere potest, et separari ab invicem debent."

59 Cf. Merkelbach, *Summa Theologiae Moralis* (2. ed., Parisiis: Desclée de Brouwer et Soc., 1936), III, n. 943. Sanchez is the main proponent for this opinion (*De Sancto Matrimonii Sacramento,* lib. II, disp. 42, nn. 7-9): "Circa secundum casum, quando scilicet uterque mala fide contraxit, dubitans de impedimento . . . credo satis esse, si arbitrio prudentis rationes ita probabiles sint, ad persuadendum matrimonium valere, ut efficiant probabilem opinionem, quamvis probabilius matrimonium non tenere: quia satis est in moralibus sententiam probabilem amplecti, iuxta veriorem opinionem; quare hac opinione probabili valoris matrimonii existenti, potest uterque petere, et reddere." This view is also supported by Payen, *De Matrimonio,* I, n. 1063; Vermeersch, *Theologiae Moralis Principia, Responsa, Consilia* (3. ed., Roma: Pont. Universitá Gregoriana, 1933), IV, n. 66; Genicot-Salsmans, *Institutiones Theologiae Moralis,* II, n. 445.

60 Among the authors favoring the stricter view are St. Alphonsus. *Theologia Moralis,* lib. VI, nn. 900, 906; Lehmkuhl, *Theologia Moralis,* I, nn. 1139-1147 II, 1076; Feije, *De Impedimentis et Dispensationibus Matrimonialibus,* n. 446; Chelodi, *Ius Matrimoniale,* n. 77, nota 1; De Smet, *De*

If one party entered the marriage in good faith, and the other in bad faith, then before an investigation is made, the former (unless he becomes aware of the doubt) may both request and grant the *debitum,* the latter may not request it, but must grant it upon the request of the party in good faith.[61] After a fruitless investigation both parties may request and grant the *debitum,* according to a probable opinion.[62]

Sponsalibus et Matrimonio, n. 238; Kaas, *Kriegsverschollenheit und Wiederverheiratung,* p. 119.

[61] "Si vero aliquis vel aliqua id hactenus non servavit, et de morte prioris coniugis adhuc sibi existimat dubitandum: ei quae sibi nupsit, debitum non deneget postulanti, quod a se tamen noverit nullatenus exigendum." Lucius III—c. 2, X, *de secundis nuptiis,* IV, 21. "Si eorum alter dubius et anceps est, reddere quidem debitum potest, non autem petere." S. C. de Prop. Fide, instr. a. 1792—*Fontes,* n. 997.

[62] Sanchez, *De Sancto Matrimonii Sacramento,* lib. II, disp. 46, n. 2; St. Alphonsus, *Theologia Moralis,* lib. VI, n. 900.

Chapter VIII

CIVIL LAW PROVISIONS WITH REGARD TO PRESUMED DEATH

Article I. American Law

In American Civil Law the question of presumption of death is closely linked with the laws prohibiting bigamy. In England bigamy was first made a civil offence in the reign of James I in 1604.[1] Before that time it was only punishable in canon law. The law of 1604 excepted from the penalties for bigamy the person whose former husband or wife had continuously remained seven years beyond the seas, or although living within his Majesty's dominions was not known by the other to be living. Later legislation limited this exception to the case in which the first husband or wife was not known to be living and a period of seven years had elapsed. Similar legislation is to be found in most of our states, although the statutes vary in a number of points.[2] Bigamous marriages are forbidden both criminally and civilly in all fifty-one of the American jurisdictions.[3]

The statutory period of absence, marriage after which escapes the penalties against bigamous marriages, varies in the different jurisdictions; it is two years in Pennsylvania, three years in Florida, Iowa and New Hampshire; four years in Hawaii; five years in Alabama, Arizona, Arkansas, California, Colorado, Delaware, Georgia, Idaho, Illinois, Kansas, Kentucky, Louisiana, Michigan, Minnesota, Montana, Nebraska, Nevada, New Jersey, New York, North Dakota, Ohio, Oklahoma, South Dakota, Tennessee, Texas, Utah, Washington, the District of Columbia, the territory

[1] 1 Jac. 1, c. 11.

[2] Bishop, *New Commentaries on Marriage, Divorce and Separation* (6. ed., Chicago, 1891), n. 715; Schouler, *A Treatise on the Law of Marriage, Divorce, Separation and Domestic Relations* (6. ed., Albany: Matthew Bender & Co., 1921), II, n. 1128.

[3] Vernier, *American Family Laws* (Stanford University, California: Stanford University Press, 1931-1932), I, 215; the leading case in the United States on the question of bigamy is Reynolds v. United States, Supreme Court of the United States, 1878, 98 U. S. 145, 25 L. Ed. 244.

of Alaska; seven years in Maine, Maryland, Massachusetts, Mississippi, Missouri, North Carolina, Oregon, Rhode Island, South Carolina, Vermont, Virginia, West Virginia, Wisconsin; although no special period is mentoned the common law period of seven is also in force in Connecticut, Indiana, New Mexico and Wyoming.[4] As a rule the statutory period of the criminal law is also used when the presumption of death is accepted for the civil effects of marriage. In Pennsylvania, however, although the statutory period exempting from prosecution in criminal law is two years, as to the civil effects death is not presumed until the lapse of seven years.[5]

It is important, though, to distinguish carefully between the criminal and the civil law effects of the presumption of death after the statutory period has elapsed. Although a person is no longer liable to the penalties of the criminal law when this period has passed, it by no means follows that his second marriage is valid. The common law rule is that, so long as a first marriage is undissolved, the second is void, even though by reason of an exception in the statute against polygamy, the individual entering it should be exempt from the penalties for bigamy.[6] "The fundamental doctrine of Christian marriage is that no length of separation can dissolve the union, so long as both parties are actually living, even though lapse of time should raise a reasonable supposition of death."[7] Therefore according to the basic principle of the common law, even though a spouse enters a new marriage, after the statutory period has elapsed, in good faith with a full but erroneous belief that the other spouse is dead, the marriage is not valid.[8] This common law principle is followed by the statutes

[4] Vernier, *op. cit.,* I, 212-222.

[5] Burr v. Sim, 4 Wharton 150 (1838); Mutual Benefit Co.'s Petition, 174 Pa. 1 (1896).

[6] Bishop, *Marriage,* I, n. 717. Cf. Goset v. Goset, 112 Ark. 47, 164 S. W. 759, L. R. A. 1916 C, 707.

[7] Schouler, *The Law of Marriage,* II, n. 1126.

[8] Glass v. Glass, Supreme Judicial Court of Massachusetts, 1874, 114 Mass. 563. In this case the parties to the second marriage had contracted the marriage in good faith with the full belief that the first

of a majority of the states,[9] and in a number of cases courts have held that such marriages are void *ab initio* where the first spouse is actually living at the time of the second marriage.[10]

However, at the present time there are seven states (California, Idaho, Minnesota, Montana, North Dakota, South Carolina, and South Dakota) which provide that when one of the spouses of a former marriage has been absent and has not been heard from for a certain period of years the second marriage is voidable only,[11] that is, it will be considered valid in law until dissolved upon petition of one of the parties concerned.[12] New York had a similar statute until 1922.[13] Arkansas goes even farther by providing that in the case where a spouse has been absent and unheard of for five years a subsequent marriage "shall be valid as if such husband or wife were dead." Louisiana and Tennessee both have statutes providing that after the statutory period elapses (ten years in this instance in Louisiana, five years in Tennessee), the first marriage shall be considered as dissolved. In addition Tennessee and Pennsylvania have statutes by virtue of which, when a spouse remarries believing the first husband or wife dead, and the latter returns after a two year period, the returning spouse has the right after

spouse was dead; nevertheless on the reappearance of the latter and on the petition of the second husband the second marriage was declared null. The common law rule is well expressed in the opinion, Martins' Heirs v. Martin, 22 Ala. 86, as follows: "Though a man marries ever so often, he can have but one lawful wife living. So long as she is living, and the marriage bond remains in full force, all his subsequent marriages whether meretricious or founded in mistake and at the same time supposed to be lawful are utterly null and void."

9 Vernier, *American Family Laws,* I, 216.

10 Jacobs, *Cases and Other Materials on Domestic Relations* (2. ed., Chicago: The Foundation Press, Inc., 1939), p. 241.

11 Vernier, *op. cit.,* I, 216.

12 Bishop, *Marriage,* I, n. 283.

13 Many of the important judicial decisions on the question of presumption of death are New York cases. Cf. especially *In re* Del Genovese's Will (1907), 107 N. Y. Supp. 1033, and Gall v. Gall, 114 N. Y. 109, 21 N. E. 106. In these cases the court held that such marriages are to be considered valid until nullified by the decree of a competent tribunal. Cf. also Bishop, *ibidem.*

proper proceedings, either to take his former spouse back, or be free to contract another marriage.[14] In other states not having such statutes some courts have pronounced marriages entered after absence of the first husband or wife as valid, saying nothing about the right of the first husband or wife to annul the subsequent marriage.[15]

In all cases where a presumption of death is admitted by the court good faith is required. A reasonable investigation to find out whether the absent person is still living is also demanded.[16]

The most important factor in the question of presumption of death with regard to freedom to contract a second marriage is not statutory requirements of any kind but the strong presumption in American Civil Law "that where parties live openly together as husband and wife for many years, a prior marriage of one of them to a third party has been dissolved by death or divorce." [17] Mere

[14] Vernier, *American Family Laws,* I, 216; Jacobs, *Domestic Relations,* p. 247.

[15] Strode v. Strode, 66 (3 Bush) Ky. 227, 96 Am. Dec. 211; Inhabitants of Hiram v. Pierce, 45 Me. 367, 71 Am. Dec. 555; Woods v. Woods Adm'rs, 2 Bay (S. C.) 476. Cf. *Mich. L. Rev.,* VI (1908), 513-514. This viewpoint is expressed in a recent decision: "It seems to us that, when the period of absence has existed for seven years, the absent party not being heard from during that time, and the presumption being that he is dead, and the wife having acted upon such presumption in good faith and contracted another marriage, such marriage is legal. To hold otherwise in this case would be to convict five persons of adultery, and would bastardize three innocent children. If the law itself acts upon the presumption, we see no reason why a party acting upon it in good faith, by contracting an irrevocable status affecting the honor and legitimacy of other people, should not so act and such act be valid. . . . It seems to us that it would be sounder reasoning to hold that, if the absence had been for the statutory period, without the party having been heard from, and a marriage having been contracted on the strength of such prolonged absence, it should be protected and the contracting parties given a valid legal status."—Harper v. Fears, 168 Miss. 505, 151 So. 745, 93 A. L. R. 341 (1934).

[16] Gall v. Gall, 114 N. Y. 109, 21 N. E. 106 (1889); Stokes v. Stokes, 198 N. Y. 310, 91 N. E. 793; Frankish v. Frankish, 206 App. Div. 301, 200 N. Y. S. 667 (1923). The degree of diligence required for the investigation by the court in the last case was "to leave no stone unturned."

[17] Schouler, *The Law of Marriage,* II, n. 1252; McLaughlin v. McLaughlin (Ala.), 78 So. 388; Goset v. Goset, 112 Ark. 47, 164 S. W. 759.

proof that a former marriage was contracted will not overcome the presumption that the second marriage is valid.[18] The American Civil Law will presume where a second marriage exists, and the statutory period has elapsed, that the first marriage has been dissolved by death. If it should be established that the first spouse is still living, the law will then presume that the marriage has been dissolved by divorce.[19] The burden of proving that a first marriage exists and has not been dissolved lies therefore on the party attacking the second marriage.[20]

It should be noted also that after the statutory period has elapsed, and the first spouse is absent and unheard from, the second marriage will be considered valid *ab initio,* even though this marriage took place before the statutory period had elapsed, since the presumption of death from absence does not give rise to a presumption of death at any particular time.[21]

[18] Lewis v. Lewis (Okla.), 158 Pac. 368.

[19] "A reasonably uniform line of reasoning has led to a widely adopted rule that all presumptions respecting marriage shift to the second and most recent marriage shown; and the previous one is presumed to have been dissolved. . . . If the death of the former spouse may not be presumed, because of sufficient evidence of his continued life, courts presume that the prior marriage has been dissolved by divorce."—*U. of Pa. L. Rev.,* LXXXII (1933-1934), 510-511. This viewpoint is well expressed in Chancey v. Whinnery, 47 Okla. 272, 147 Pac. 1036 (1915): "So strong is the presumption and the law is so positive in requiring the party who asserts the illegality of a marriage to take the burden of proving it, that such requirement obtains, even though it involved the proving of a negative, and although it is shown that one of the parties had contracted a previous marriage, and the existence of the wife or husband is established by proof, it is not sufficient to overcome the presumption of the validity of the second marriage, the law presuming rather that the first marriage has been dissolved by divorce, in order to sustain the second marriage." This statement is quoted with approval in later decisions, for example, Lathan v. Lathan, 175 Ark. 1037, 1 S. W. (2nd) 67; Spears v. Spears, Supreme Court of Arkansas, 1928, 178 Ark. 720, 12 S. W. (2nd) 875.

[20] Patterson v. Gaines, 6 How. U. S. 550, 592; Gaines v. Hennen, 24 How. U. S. 553. Cf. Bishop, *Marriage,* I, n. 720.

[21] Smith v. Fuller, 108 N. W. 765 (Iowa, 1906); Johnson v. Johnson, 114 Ill. 611, 3 N. E. 232 (1885).

The practice in American Civil Law is that the presumption of the validity of a second marriage overrules the presumption of continuance of life. In any conflict between the two the former will invariably be upheld.[22]

Previous to 1922 in New York a marriage after five years' absence of the first spouse with probability of death was considered voidable.[23] In 1922 the law was amended so that the first marriage in cases of this kind will be dissolved upon proof that the first spouse has been absent for five years and is not known to be living; provided that the husband or wife making the petition believes the absent party to be dead, and has made a diligent though fruitless search to discover whether or not the absent spouse is alive.[24] By a decision of a higher court in 1931 (with two justices dissenting), it has been decided that in cases of this kind it is not necessary that the court itself should be convinced that the person is dead, but only that the petitioner in good faith believes that the absent spouse is dead.[25]

In four states a divorce can be obtained for the reason that a spouse has been absent and unheard from: Connecticut (seven years), New Hampshire (three years), Rhode Island ("from

[22] "Much of the difficulty with this presumption [presumption that a second marriage is valid] has centered around the supposed conflict between it and 'the presumption of continuance of life,' no presumption at all, but an inference which may be barred by the presumption of death in order to validate the second marriage. The spurious presumption 'of continuance of life' is always held to have been overcome."—*U. of Pa. L. Rev.*, LXXXII (1933-1934), 511.

[23] Cf. *supra*, p. 123.

[24] Jacobs, *Domestic Relations*, p. 243.

[25] "What is made of controlling importance is the good faith of the petitioner in bringing the proceeding and in believing that his wife was dead, together with the proof of the exercise of proper diligence by him in an effort to locate her and find proof that she is alive. The jurisdictional facts being sufficiently shown, all that petitioner was required to do was to satisfy the court of the truth of all the allegations contained in the petition."—*In re* Heilwell, 232 App. Div. 610, 250 N. Y. S. 670 (1931). Cf. also *In the matter of* Entenman, 112 Misc. 441, 204 N. Y. S. 100 (1924); Frankish v. Frankish, 206 App. Div. 301, 200 N. Y. S. 667 (1923).

absence or other circumstances may be presumed to be actually dead"), Vermont (seven years).[26]

The official declaration of death as such, which is so important in Canon Law and in Continental Civil Law with regard to freedom to contract a second marriage, seems to have but little significance in American Civil Law; such a declaration would have no more effect than the private opinion of the parties themselves based on good faith and formed after a reasonable investigation.[27]

When parties have entered in good faith a marriage which was void because of the impediment of a previous marriage of one of them, the second marriage will be validated by the removal of the impediment and by the continued cohabitation of the parties. For this validation to take place it is necessary that the parties have been living together as man and wife and intended a marriage contract.[28] If in such a case only one of the parties was in good faith, the other being aware that the first marriage was not dissolved, there is a sharp division of opinion, with a slight majority of judicial decisions holding that continued cohabitation will suffice to permit findng a new contract.[29] Four jurisdictions (Alaska, Iowa, Massachusetts and Wisconsin) have statutes providing that when a prohibited bigamous marriage was contracted in good faith by one of the parties, if they continue to live together (in good

[26] Vernier, *American Family Laws,* II, 70. Divorce is obtainable in seven states when the parties have been living apart for a term of years: Kentucky (five years), Louisiana (seven years), North Carolina (five years), Rhode Island (ten years), Texas (ten years), Washington (five years), Wisconsin (five years).—Vernier, *ibidem.* In addition forty-seven jurisdictions allow divorce for wilful desertion.—Vernier, *op. cit.,* II, 31.

[27] This viewpoint is well expressed in *In re* Kotlik's Estate, Surrogate's Court of King's County, New York (1934), 153 Misc. 355, 274 N. Y. S. 838: "Whereas, therefore, the procurement of such an adjudication [declaration of death by a court] may be a wise precautionary measure averting unpleasant consequences if the absentee reappears, it has no further or greater utility, and unless or until the reappearance of the absentee, is wholly futile and meaningless, amounting merely to an asseveration by a tribunal of a belief which the applicant presumably already entertains."

[28] Schouler, *The Law of Marriage,* II, n. 1129.

[29] *U. of Pa. L. Rev.,* LXXXII (1933-1934), 513.

faith on the part of one of them) after the impediment has been removed, the second marriage will be considered legal from and after the removal of the impediment. The Iowa statute does not expressly require good faith on the part of either party.[30] When both parties have contracted marriage with the knowledge that a prior marriage was still in existence, in order that a marriage will be presumed after the removal of the impediment, some evidence of a change of attitude or of a new and valid agreement is required.[31] [32]

Article II. Continental Civil Law

The German civil code (§ § 13-18) provides for a declaration of death in regard to a person who has been absent and unheard of for a period of ten years and who is at least 31 years of age. However, if the missing person is over 70 years of age a declaration of death will be issued after five years of absence. For a person missing in war the statutory period is three years computed from the time that peace is declared; for a person missing after shipwreck, one to three years, depending on whether the shipwreck took place in near or distant waters; for other disasters: explosions, earthquakes and the likes: three years from the time of the disaster.[33] However, on the 18th of April, 1916, special provisions were made by the German government for cases arising out of the World War; a declaration of death could be issued one year after a soldier was missing.[34] According to the German civil code

[30] Vernier, *American Family Laws,* I, 216.

[31] *U of Pa. L. Rev.,* LXXXII (1933-1934), 513.

[32] A comparison of the Canon Law and American Civil Law requirements for presumption of death of a prior spouse with regard to freedom to contract a new marriage is made by Alford, *Jus Matrimoniale Comparatum* (Roma: Anonima Libraria Cattolica Italiana, 1938), nn. 122-126.

[33] Kaas, *Kriegsverschollenheit und Wiederverheiratung,* p. 21. Cf. also Linneborn, *Grundriss des Eherechts,* p. 193; Triebs, *Handbuch des kanonischen Eherechts,* p. 317.

[34] Kaas, *op. cit.,* p. 25. On April 26, 1917, the Prince Bishop of Breslau warned his priests that the presumption of death after one year by the civil authorities (by the decree of April 18, 1916) in the case of missing

(§ § 1348-1350), a second marriage contracted after a declaration of death is valid, even if the missing person returns, provided that the marriage was entered in good faith. If the missing person reappears, the spouse who remarried has the right to attack the second marriage and to have the first marriage reinstated, provided that this right be exercised within six months of the time at which knowledge was first obtained concerning the fact that the first spouse was still alive. The returning party, however, has the right to attack the second marriage only when it was contracted in bad faith.[35]

According to the Italian civil code, death is proved by an official certificate, by other documents or by witnesses. The provisions of the law with regard to absence refer only to property questions (Art. 362, 364), and permission to remarry is not granted by reason of absence of one's spouse (Art. 20-47). However, if the spouse of an absent person should remarry illegally, the second marriage cannot be attacked, as long as the first spouse is still missing (Art. 113). Special regulations were issued on April 15, 1919, for the cases arising out of the World War, according to which the following were presumed dead:

a) those who disappeared in the course of a battle and were still missing one year after the war ended; b) those missing for one year after a shipwreck; c) persons taken prisoner by the enemy, concerning whom nothing to indicate life or death has been heard for three years. The Italian civil declaration of death in the above cases is purely declaratory, and on the reappearance of the missing person the second marriage is considered null.[36]

In France, the civil code provides for proof of death by an official certificate, by other documents or by witnesses (Art. 46). A presumption of death is admitted in the case of those who disap-

soldiers did not suffice for the Church, but that they were bound by the instruction of 1868; that the pastor could proceed only when an authentic official certificate of death, whether ecclesiastic or civil, was present. In other cases the pastor was to gather up the evidence and send the case to the Curia.—*AKKR,* XCVII (1917), 441.

[35] Kaas, *Kriegsverschollenheit und Wiederverheiratung,* pp. 32-36.

[36] Chelodi, *Ius Matrimoniale,* n. 78.

peared in connection with a shipwreck (Art. 89-91). On Dec. 3, 1915, this provision was extended to those missing in the World War. A period of four years' absence without news is required before death may be presumed in such cases (Art. 115). The second marriage in a case of presumed death may be attacked only by the missing spouse on his return.[37]

[37] Chelodi, *Ius Matrimoniale*, n. 78.

CONCLUSIONS

The following conclusions derived from the foregoing study are either findings on points not previously considered by canonists since the Code, or are the results of a more thorough investigation than that usually given by the authors to this topic:

1. Proof of death by presumptions alone was not permitted by the Sacred Congregations until the latter part of the eighteenth century.

2. The competence of the Ordinary for an administrative process with regard to the proof of death of a former spouse will be determined not by canons 1561 or 1964, but by canon 201.

3. When judicial procedure is used for the process for proof of death, one judge will suffice, for a tribunal of three judge is required only in marriage cases affecting the bond of marriage.

4. In the administrative process for proof of death recourse is permissible to the Sacred Congregation of the Sacraments, but not to the Metropolitan nor to the Rota.

5. Except in the case where the pastor has personal knowledge of the death of a spouse or possesses an authentic death certificate, all cases involving the proof of death of a husband or wife belong to the competence of the Ordinary.

6. In danger of death the pastor may assist at a marriage, in accordance with the provisions of canon 1019, § 2, if the parties themselves have personal knowledge of the death of the first spouse of either of them, or if they had received official authentic notification of the death of the person in question, provided that the conditions mentioned in this canon are fufilled.

APPENDIX

Instruction of the Sacred Congregation of the Holy Office
May 13, 1868 — *Fontes, n.* 1002

Matrimonii vinculo duos tantummodo, Christo ita docente, copulari et coniungi posse; alterutro vero coniuge vita functo, secundas, imo et ulteriores nuptias licitas esse, dogmatica Ecclesiae catholicae doctrina est.

Verum ad secundas et ulteriores nuptias quod attinet, cum de re agatur quae difficultatibus ac fraudibus haud raro est obnoxia, hinc Sancta Sedes sedulo curavit, modo constitutionibus generalibus, saepius autem responsis in casibus particularibus datis, ut libertas novas nuptias ineundi ita cuique salva esset, ut praedicta matrimonii unitas in discrimen non adduceretur.

Inde constituta sacrorum Canonum quibus, ut quis possit licite ad alia vota transire, exigitur quod de morte coniugis certo constet, uti cap. *Dominus, De secundis nuptiis,* vel quod de ipsa morte recipiatur *certum nuncium,* uti cap. *In praesentia, De sponsalibus et matrimoniis.* Inde etiam ea quae explanatius traduntur in instructione *"Cum Alias,"* 21 Augusti 1670, a Clemente X sancita, et in Bullario Romano inserta super examine testium pro matrimoniis contrahendis in Curia Emi Vicarii Urbis et caeterorum Ordinariorum. Maxime vero quae propius ad rem facientia ibi habentur nn. 12 et 13.

Et haec quidem abunde sufficerent si in eiusmodi causis peragendis omnimoda et absoluta certitudo de alterius coniugis obitu haberi semper posset; sed cum id non sinant casuum propemodum infinitae vices (quod sapienter animadversum est in laudata Instructione his verbis: *Si tamen huiusmodi testimonia haberi non possunt, Sacra Congregatio non intendit excludere alias probationes, quae de iure communi possunt admittis dummodo legitimae sint et sufficientes)* sequitur, quod stantibus licet principiis generalibus praestitutis, haud raro casus eveniunt, in quibus ecclesiasticorum praesidum iudicia haerere solent in vera iustaque probatione dignoscenda ac statuenda, imo pro summa illa facilitate quae aetate nostra facta est, remotissimas quasque regiones adeundi, ita ut in omnes fere orbis partes homines divagentur, eiusmodi casuum multitudo adeo succrevit, ut frequentissimi hac de re ad Supremam hanc Congr. habentur recursus non sine porro partium incommodo, quibus inter informationes atque instructiones, quas pro re nata, ut aiunt, peti mittique necesse est, plurimum defluit temporis quin possint ad optata vota convolare.

Quapropter Sacra eadem Congr. huiusmodi necessitatibus occurrere percupiens, simulque perpendens in dissitis praesertim Missionum locis ecclesiasticos praesides opportunis destitui subsidiis, quibus ex gravibus difficultatibus extricare se valeant, e re esse censuit, uberiorem edere Instructionem in qua, iis, quae iam tradita sunt, nullo pacto abrogatis, regulae indigitentur, quas in eiusmodi casibus haec ipsa S. Congr. sequi solet, ut illarum ope, vel absque necessitate recursus ad Sanctam Sedam possint iudicia ferri: vel certe, si recurrendum sit, status questionis ita dilucide exponatur, ut impediri longiori mora sententia non debeat. Itaque:

1. Cum de coniugis morte quaestio instituitur, notandum primo loco quod argumentum a sola ipsius absentia quantacumque (licet a legibus civilibus fere ubique admittatur) a sacris canonibus minime sufficiens ad iustam probationem habetur. Unde sa. me. Pius VI ad Archiep. Pragensem die 11 Iulii 1789 rescripsit solam coniugis absentiam atque omnimodum eiusdem silentium *satis argumentum non esse ad mortem comprobandam,* ne tum quidem cum edicto regio coniux absens evocatus (idemque porro dicendum est, si per publicas ephemerides id factum sit) nullum suimet indicium dederit. *Quod enim non comparuerit,* idem ait Pontifex, *non magis mors in causa esse potuit, quam eius contumacia.*

2. Hinc ad praescriptum eorumdem sacrorum Canonum, documentum authenticum obitus diligenti studio exquiri omnino debet; exaratum scilicet ex regestis paroeciae, vel xenodochii, vel militiae, vel etiam, si haberi nequeat ab auctoritate ecclesiastica, a gubernio civili loci in quo, ut supponitur, persona obierit.

3. Porro quandoque hoc documentum haberi nequit; quo casu testium depositionibus supplendum erit. Testes vero duo saltem esse debent, iurati, fide digni, et qui de facto proprio deponat, defunctum cognoverint, ac sint inter se concordes quoad locum, et causam obitus aliasque substantiales circumstantias. Qui in-

super, si defuncti propinqui sint, aut socii itineris, industriae, vel etiam militiae, eo magis plurimi faciendum erit illorum testimonium.

4. Interdum unus tantum testis examinandus reperitur, et licet ab omni iure testimonium unius ad plene probandum non admittatur, attamen ne coniux alias nuptias inire peroptans vitam coelibem agere cogatur, etiam unius testimonium absolute non respuit Suprema Cong. in dirimendis huiusmodi casibus, dummodo ille testis, recensitis conditionibus sit praeditus, nulli exceptioni obnoxius, ac praeterea eius depositio alliis gravibusque adminiculis fulciatur: sique alia extrinseca adminicula colligi omnino nequeant, hoc tamen certum sit, nihil in eius testimonio reperiri quod non sit congruum atque omnino verisimile.

5. Contigit etiam ut testes omnimoda fide digni testificentur se tempore non suspecto mortem coniugis ex aliorum attestatione audivisse, isti autem vel quia absentes, vel quia obierint vel aliam ob quamcumque rationabilem causam examinari nequeunt; tunc dicta ex alieno ore, quatenus omnibus aliis in casu concurrentibus circumstantiis, aut saltem urgentibus respondeant, satis esse censentur pro sequutae mortis prudenti iudicio.

6. Verum, haud semel experientia compertum habetur, quod nec unus quidem reperiatur testis qualis supra adstruitur. Hoc in casu probatio obitus ex coniecturis, praesumptionibus, indiciis et adiunctis quibuscumque, sedula certe et admodum cauta investigatione curanda erit, ita nimirum ut pluribus hinc inde collectis, eorumque natura perpensa, prout scilicet urgentiora vel leviora sunt, seu propiore vel remotiore nexu cum veritate mortis coniunguntur, inde prudentis viri iudicium ad eamdem mortem affirmandam probabilitate maxima, seu morali certitudine promoveri possit. Quapropter quandonam in singulis casibus habeatur ex huiusmodi coniecturis simul coniunctis iusta probatio, id prudenti relinquendum est iudicis arbitrio; heic tamen non abs re erit plures indicare fontes ex quibus illae sive urgentiores, sive etiam leviores colligi et haberi possint.

7. Itaque in primis illae praesumptiones investigandae erunt quae personam ipsius asserti defuncti respiciunt, quaeque profecto facile haberi poterunt a coniunctis, amicis, vicinis, et quoque

modo notis utriusque coniugis. In quorum examine requiratur, ex. gr.:—

An ille, de cuius obitus est sermo, bonis moribus imbutus esset, pie religioseque viveret, uxoremque diligeret; nullam sese occultandi causam haberet; utrum bona stabilia possideret, vel alia a suis propinquis aut aliunde sperare posset.

An discesserit, annuentibus uxore et coniunctis; quae tunc eius aetas, et valetudo esset. An aliquando et quo loco scripserit, et num suam voluntatem quamprimum redeundi aperuerit, aliaque huius generis indicia colligantur.

Alia ex rerum adiunctis pro varia absentiae causà colligi indicia sic poterunt:—

Si ob militiam abierit, a duce militum requiratur quid de eo sciat; utrum alicui pugnae interfuerit; utrum ab hostibus fuerit captus; num castra deseruerit, aut destinationes periculosas habuerit etc.

Si negotiationis causa iter susceperit, inquiratur, utrum tempore itineris gravia pericula fuerint ipsi superanda; num solus profectus fuerit, vel pluribus comitatus; utrum in regionem ad quam se contulit supervenerint seditiones, bella, fames et pestilentiae etc.

Si maritimum iter fuerit aggressus, sedula investigatio fiat a quo portu discesserit; quinam fuerint itineris socii; quo se contulerit; quod nomen navis quam conscendit; quis eiusdem navis gubernator; an naufragium fecerit; an societas, quae navis cautionem forsan dedit, pretium eius solverit; aliaeque circumstantiae, si quae sint, diligenter perpendantur.

8. Fama quoque aliis adiuta adminiculis argumentum de obitu constituit, hisce tamen conditionibus, nimirum: quod a duobus saltem testibus fide dignis et iuratis comprobetur, qui deponant de rationabili causa ipsius famae: an eam acceperint a maiori et saniori parte populi, et an ipsi de eadem fama recte sentiant; nec sit dubium illam fuisse concitatam ab illis in quorum commodum inquiritur.

9. Tandem, si opus fuerit, praetereunda non erit investigatio per publicas ephemerides, datis directori omnibus necessariis personae indiciis, nisi ob speciales circumstantias saniori ac prudentiori consilio aliter censeatur.

10. Haec omnia pro opportunitate casuum Sacra haec Congr. diligenter expendere solet, cumque de re gravissima agatur, cunctis aequa lance libratis, atque insuper auditis plurium theologorum et iurisprudentum suffragiis, denique suum iudicium pronunciat an de tali obitu satis constet, et nihil obstet quominus petenti transitus ad alias nuptias concedi possit.

11. Ex his omnibus ecclesiastici praesides certam desumere possunt normam quam in huiusmodi iudiciis sequantur. Quod si non obstantibus regulis hucusque notatis, res adhuc incerta et implexa illis videatur, ad S. Sedem recurrere debebunt, actis omnibus cum ipso recursu transmissis, aut saltem diligenter expositis.*

* The instruction of 1868 will be found also in *Collectanea,* II, n. 1321; *ASS,* VI (1870), 434-441; *Acta et Decreta Concilii Plenarii Baltimorensis Tertii* (1884), pp. 258-261; *AAS,* II (1910), 199-203.

BIBLIOGRAPHY

Sources

Acta Apostolicae Sedis, Commentarium Officiale, Romae, 1909—

Acta et Decreta Sacrorum Conciliorum Recentiorum Collectio Lacensis, Friburgi Brisgoviae, 1870-1890.

Acta Sanctae Sedis, 41 vols., Romae, 1865-1908.

Bullarum Diplomatum et Privilegiorum Sanctorum Romanorum Pontificum Taurinensis Editio, 25 vols., Augustae Taurinorum, 1857-1872.

Codex Iuris Canonici Pii X Pontificis Maximi iussu digestus Benedicti Papae XV auctoritate promulgatus, Romae, Typis Polyglottis Vaticanis, 1917.

Codex Iuris Canonici Fontes cura Emi Petri Card. Gasparri editi, 9 vols., Romae (later Civitate Vaticano) :—Typis Polyglottis Vaticanis, 1923-1939. (Vols. VII, VIII et. IX ed. *cura et studio Emi Iustiniani Card. Serédi.*)

Collectanea S. Congregationis de Propaganda Fide, 2 vols., Romae: Typographia Polyglotta S. C. de Propaganda Fide, 1907.

Concilii Plenarii Baltimorensis II., in Ecclesia Metropolitana Baltimorensi, a die VII. ad diem XXI. Octobris, A.D. MDCCCLXVI., Habiti, et a Sede Apostolica Recogniti, Acta et Decreta, Baltimorae: John Murphy, 1868.

Concilium Tridentinum, Diariorum, Actorum, Epistolarum, Tractatum, Nova Collectio. Edidit Societas Goerresiana. 9 vols., Friburgi Brisgoviae: B. Herder, 1901-1930.

Corpus Iuris Canonici, Editio Lipsiensis II (Richter-Friedberg), 2 vols., Lipsiae, 1922.

Corpus Iuris Civilis, 3 vols., Berolini, 1928-1929.
Institutiones, quas recognovit P. Krueger;
Digesta, quae recognovit et retractavit P. Krueger;
Codex Iustinianus, quem recognovit et retractavit P. Krueger;
Novellae, quas recognovit R. Schoell, et absolvit G. Kroll.

Decretales D. Gregorii Papae IX, una cum Glossis Restitutae, Romae, 1582.

Denzinger, Henr., et Bannwart, Clem., *Enchiridion Symbolorum, Definitionum et Declarationum de Rebus Fidei et Morum,* 16. et 17. ed., Friburgi Brisgoviae: Herder, 1928.

Friedberg, Aemilius, *Quinque Compilationes Antiquae,* Lipsiae, 1882.

Haddan, Arthur West, and Stubbs, William, *Councils and Ecclesiastical Documents relating to Great Britain and Ireland,* 3 vols., Oxford, 1869-1873.

Hartzheim, *Concilia Germaniae,* 11 vols., Coloniae Augustae Agrippinensium, 1759-1790.

Jaffé, Philippus, *Regesta Pontificum Romanorum ab condita Ecclesia ad annum post Christum natum MCXCVIII,* 2 vols. in 1, Lipsiae, 1885-1888.

Mansi, Joannes, *Sacrorum Conciliorum Nova et Amplissima Collectio,* 53 vols., Parisiis, 1901-1927.

Migne, Jacques Paul, *Patrologiae Cursus Completus, Series Graeca,* 161 vols., Parisiis, 1856-1866.

————, *Patrologiae Cursus Completus, Series Latina,* 221 vols., Parisiis, 1844-1864.

Monumenta Germaniae Historica, Legum Sectio II, Capitularia Regum Francorum, Tom. I, ed. A. Boretino, Hannoverae, 1883.

Monumenta Germaniae Historica, Leges, 5 vols., Lipsiae, 1925.

Pallottini, Salvator, *Collectio Omnium Conclusionum et Resolutionum Quae in causis propositis apud Sacram Congregationem Cardinalium S. Concilii Tridentini Interpretum Prodierunt ab eius institutione anno MDLXIX ad annum MDCCCLX, distinctis titulis alphabetico ordine per materias digesta,* 17 vols., Romae, 1868-1893.

S. Romanae Rotae Decisiones seu Sententiae quae . . . prodierunt anno 1909-1931, 23 vols., Romae: Typis Vaticanis, 1912-1939.

Thesaurus Resolutionum Sacrae Congregationis Concilii, 167 vols., Romae, 1718-1908.

Reference Works

Alford, Culver Bernard, *Jus Matrimoniale Comparatum,* Roma: Anonima Libraria Cattolica Italiana, 1938.

Aquinas, Thomas, *Opera Omnia, Vol. VII, Commentum in Quattuor Libros Sententiarum,* Parmae, 1856.

Ayrinhac-Lydon, *Marriage Legislation in the New Code of Canon Law,* new, revised edition, New York, Benziger Brothers, 1938.

[Bachofen], Charles Augustine, *A Commentary on the New Code of Canon Law,* 4. ed., 8 vols., St. Louis: B. Herder, 1921-1929.

Bellarmine, Robertus, *Opera Omnia,* Tom. III, *De Sacramento Matrimonii,* Venetiis, 1721.

Billot, Louis, *De Ecclesiae Sacramentis,* 2 vols. in 1, Romae, 1891.

Bishop, J. P., *New Commentaries on Marriage, Divorce and Separation,* 6. ed., 2 vols., Chicago. 1891.

Bouscaren, T. Lincoln, *The Canon Law Digest,* 2 vols., and Supplement—1938, Milwaukee: Bruce, 1934-1937.

Bouix, D., *Tractatus de Iudiciis Ecclesiasticis,* 2. ed., 2 vols., Parisiis, 1855.

Brennan, James H., *The Simple Convalidation of Marriage,* The Catholic University of America, Canon Law Studies, n. 102, Washington: The Catholic University of America, 1937.

Buckland, W.W., *A Textbook of Roman Law from Augustus to Justinian,* 2. ed., Cambridge: University Press, 1932.

Cappello, Felix M., *Tractatus Canonico-Moralis de Sacramentis,* Vol. III, *De Matrimonio,* 4. ed., Romae: Apud Aedes Univ. Gregorianae, 1939.

Cerato, P., *Matrimonium a codice I.C. integre Desumptum,* 4. ed., Patavii: Libr. Gregoriana edidit typis Seminarii, 1927.

Chelodi, Ioannis, *Ius Matrimoniale,* 4. ed., recognita et aucta a Vigilio Dalpiaz, Tridenti: Libreria Moderna Editrice A. Ardesi, 1937.

Cicognani, Amleto Giovanni, *Canon Law,* 2. ed., Philadelphia: The Dolphin Press, 1935.

Coffey, P., *The Science of Logic,* 2 vols., New York: Peter Smith, 1938. (First published 1912, reprinted 1938 by special arrangement with Longmans, Green & Co., London.)

Connolly, Thomas A., *Appeals,* The Catholic University of America, Canon Law Studies, n. 79, Washington: The Catholic University of America, 1932.

Corbett, Percy E., *The Roman Law of Marriage,* Oxford: Clarendon Press, 1930.

Covarruvias, Didacus, *Opera Omnia,* 2 vols., Genevae, 1762.

A Coronata, Matthaeus, *Institutiones Iuris Canonici,* 5 vols. (Vols. I et. II, 2. ed.), Taurini: Marietti, 1933-1939.

De Becker, Iulius, *De Matrimonio Praelectiones Canonicae,* ed. nova, Louvain: Fr. Ceuterick, 1931.

De Smet, Al., *Tractatus Theologico-Çanonicus De Sponsalibus et Matrimonio,* 4. ed., Brugis: Car. Beyaert, 1927.

Doheny, William J., *Canonical Procedure in Matrimonial Cases,* Milwaukee: Bruce, 1938.

Donohue, John F., *The Impediment of Crime,* The Catholic University of America, Canon Law Studies, n. 69, Washington: The Catholic University of America, 1931.

Donovan, James J., *The Pastor's Obligation in Pre-Nuptial Investigation,* The Catholic University of America, Canon Law Studies, n. 115, Washington: The Catholic University of America, 1938.

Durandus a Sancto Porciano, *In Petri Lombardi Sententias Theologicas Commentariorum libri IV,* Venetiis, 1586.

Esmein, A., *Le Mariage en Droit Canonique,* 2. ed., 2 vols., Paris: Recueil Sirey, 1929-1935.

Fahrner, Ignaz, *Geschichte der Eheschdeidung im kanonischen Recht,* Freiburg im Breisgau, 1903.

Feije, Henricus J., *De Impedimentis et Dispensationibus Matrimonialibus,* 3. ed., 2 vols., Lovanii, 1885.

Fourneret, Pierre, *Le Mariage Chrétien,* 4. ed., Paris: Gabriel Beauchesne, 1925.

Fournier, Paul—Le Bras, Gabriel, *Histoire des Collections Canoniques en Occident,* 2 vols., Paris: Recueil Sirey, 1931.

Freisen, Joseph, *Geschichte des Canonischen Eherechts,* 2. ed., Paderborn. 1893.

Gasparri, Petrus, *Tractatus Canonicus de Matrimonio,* 3. ed., 2 vols., Romae, 1904.

————, *Tractatus Canonicus de Matrimonio,* ed. nova, ad mentem Codicis I.C., 2 vols., Romae: Typis Polyglottis Vaticanis, 1932.

Genicot, Eduardus, *Institutiones Theologiae Moralis,* 11. ed., 2 vols., quam recognovit I. Salsmans, Bruxellis: Alb. Dewit, 1927.

Gerson Jean, *Opera Omnia,* Tom. III, *Regulae Morales,* Antwerp, 1706.

Giraldi, Ubaldus, *Expositio Iuris Pontificii,* 2 vols., Romae, 1830.

Gonzales-Tellez, Emmanuel, *Commentaria Perpetua in Singulos Textus Quinque Librorum Decretalium Gregorii IX,* 5 vols. in 4, Lugduni, 1715.

Haring, Johann B., *Grundzüge des katholischen Kirchenrechtes,* 3. ed., 2 vols., Graz: Ulrich Mosers Buchhandlung, 1924.

Hefele, Carolus et Leclercq, Henricus, *Histoire des Conciles,* 10 vols. in 19, Paris, 1907-1938.

Hostiensis, Cardinalis (Henricus de Segusio), *Commentaria in Quinque Decretalium Libros,* 5 vols. in 3, Venetiis, 1581.

————, *Summa Aurea,* Lugduni, 1568.

Jacobs, A.C., *Cases and Other Materials on Domestic Relations,* 2. ed., Chicago: The Foundation Press, Inc., 1939.

Joyce, George Hayward, *Christian Marriage,* Heythrop Theological Series, I, London: Sheed and Ward, 1933.

Kaas, L., *Kriegsverschollenheit und Wiederverheiratung nach staatlichem und kirchlichem Recht,* Paderborn: Ferdinand Schöningh, 1919.

Kay, Thomas H., *Competence in Matrimonial Procedure,* The Catholic University of America, Canon Law Studies, n. 53, Washington: The Catholic University of America, 1929.

Kennedy, Edwin J., *The Special Matrimonial Process in Cases of Evident Nullity,* The Catholic University of America, Canon Law Studies, n. 93, Washington: The Catholic University of America, 1935.

Kutschker, Johann, *Das Eherecht der katholischen Kirche,* 5 vols. in 4, Wien, 1856.

Lanier, Henri, *Guide Pratique de la Procédure Matrimoniale en Droit Canonique,* Paris: Pierre Tequi, 1927.

Lehmkuhl, Augustinus, *Theologia Moralis,* 11. ed., 2 vols., Friburgi Brisgoviae, 1910.

Leitner, Martin, *Lehrbuch des katholischen Eherechts,* 3. ed., Paderborn: Ferdinand Schöningh, 1920.

De Ligorio, St. Alphonsus, *Theologia Moralis,* 2 vols., Augustae Taurinorum, 1891.

Linneborn, Johannes, *Grundriss des Eherechts nach dem Codex Iuris Canonici,* 4. and 5. ed., Paderborn: Ferdinand Schöningh, 1933.

Lombardus, Petrus, *Libri IV Sententiarum,* 2. ed., 2 vols., Ad Claras Aquas prope Florentiam: Ex Typographia Collegii S. Bonaventurae, 1916.

Maasen, Friedrich, *Geschichte der Quellen und der Literatur des canonischen Rechts im Abendlande bis zum Ausgang des Mittelalters* (only one volume completed), Graz, 1870.

Manning, John J., *Presumptions of Law in Marriage Cases,* The Catholic University of America, Canon Law Studies, n. 94, Washington: The Catholic University of America, 1935.

Maroto, Philippus, *Institutiones Iuris Canonici,* Romae, 1919.

Mascardus, Joseph, *De Probationibus,* 3 vols., Venetiis, 1593.

Menochius, Jacobus, *De Praesumptionibus,* 2 vols., Coloniae Allobrogum, 1686.

Merkelbach, Benedictus Henricus, *Summa Theologiae Moralis,* 2. ed., 3 vols., Parisiis: Desclée de Brouwer et Soc., 1936.

McNeill, John T. and Gamer, Helena M., *Medieval Handbooks of Penance, Records of Civilization: Sources and Studies,* Columbia University, n. XXIX, New York: Columbia University Press, 1938.

Michiels, Gommarus, *Normae Generalis Juris Canonici,* 2 vols., Lublin, Polonia: Universitas Catholica, 1929.

Moriarty, Eugene J., *Oaths in Ecclesiastical Courts,* The Catholic University of America, Canon Law Studies, n. 110, Washington: The Catholic University of America, 1937.

Navarrus, Martinus A., *Opera Omnia,* 6 vols., Venetiis, 1618.

Noldin, H., and Schmitt, A., *Summa Theologiae Moralis,* 25. ed., 3 vols., Oeniponte: Fel. Rauch, 1938.

——————, *De Sexto Praecepto et De Usu Matrimonii,* 30. ed., Oeniponte: Fel. Rauch, 1938.

Noval, Joseph, *De Processibus,* 2 vols., Augustae Taurinorum—Romae: Marietti, 1920-1932.

Palmieri, Dominicus, *Tractatus de Matrimonio Christiano,* Romae, 1880.

Panormitanus, Abbas (Nicolaus de Tudeschis), *Commentaria in Quinque Libros Decretalium,* 5 vols. in 7, Venetiis, 1588.

Payen, G., *De Matrimonio in Missionibus Ac Potissimum in Sinis Tractatus Practicus et Casus,* 2. ed., 3 vols., Zi-Ka-wei: In typographia T'ou-sè-wè, 1935-1936.

Péries, G., *Code de Procédure Canonique dans les Causes Matrimoniales,* Paris, 1894.

Perrone, J., *De Matrimonio Christiano,* 3 vols., Romae, 1858.

Pighi J.B., *Cursus Theologiae Moralis,* 4. ed., Veronae: Sorores Cinquetti Filiae Felicis, 1926.

Pirhing, Henricus, *Ius Canonicum,* 5 vols., Dilingae, 1728.

Pitra, I.B., *Iuris Ecclesiastici Graecorum Historia et Monumenta,* 2 vols. Romae, 1864-1868.

Reiffenstuel, Anacletus, *Ius Canonicum Universum,* 4 vols., Venetiis, 1735.

Roberti, Franciscus, *De Processibus,* 2 vols., Romae: Apud Aedes Facultatis Iuridicae ad S. Appolinaris, 1926.

Sanchez, Thomas, *Disputationum de Sancto Matrimonii Sacramento Libri Tres,* Antwerp, 1626.

Santi, Franciscus and Leitner, Martinus, *Praelectiones Juris Canonici,* 5 vols., Ratisbonae, 1905.

Scherer, Rudolf Ritter von, *Handbuch des Kirchenrechtes,* 2 vols., Graz und Leipzig, 1886-1898.

Schmalzgrueber, Franciscus, *Ius Ecclesiasticum Universum,* 5 vols. in 12, Romae, 1843-1845.

Schouler, J., *A Treatise on the Law of Marriage, Divorce, Separation and Domestic Relations,* 3 vols., 6 ed., rev. by Blackmore, A. W., Albany: Matthew Bender & Co., 1921.

Singer, Heinrich, *Summa Decretorum Magistri Rufini,* Paderborn, 1902.

Thaner, Fredericus, *Anselmi Episcopi Lucensis Collectio Canonum,* Innsbruck, 1906-1915.

——————, *Summa Magistri Rolandi,* Innsbruck, 1874.

Toso, Albertus, *Ad Codicem Iuris Canonici Commentaria Minora,* 5 vols., Romae: Marietti, 1920-1934.

Triebs, Franz, *Praktisches Handbuch des geltenden kanonischen Eherechts in Vergleichung mit dem deutschen staatlichen Eherecht,* Breslau: Ostdeutsche Verlangsanstalt, 1933.

Van Hove, A., *De Legibus Ecclesiasticis,* Mechliniae—Romae: H. Dessain, 1930.

Vermeersch, Arthurus, *Theologiae Moralis Principia—Responsa—Concilia,* 3. ed., 4 vols., Roma: Pont. Universitá Gregoriana, 1933.

Vermeersch, Arthurus, and Creusen, Iosephus, *Epitome Iuris Canonici,* 3 vols. (Vol. I, 6. ed., Vols. II and III, 5. ed.), Mechliniae—Romae: H. Dessain, 1934-1937.

Vernier, C.G., *American Family Laws,* Vols. I and II, Stanford University, California: Stanford University Press, 1931-1932.

Vlaming, Th. M., *Praelectiones Iuris Matrimonii ad normam codicis iruis canonici,* 3. ed., 2 vols., Bussum in Hollandia: Sumptibus Societatis Editricis Anoymae olim Paulus Brand, 1919.

Vromant, G., *Ius Missionarium,* Vol. V, *De Matrimonio,* Louvain: Museum Lessianum 1931.

Wanenmacher, Francis, *Canonical Evidence in Marriage Cases,* Philadelphia: The Dolphin Press, 1935.

Wernz, Franciscus X. *Ius Decretalium,* 2. ed., Romae, 1908-1913.

Wernz-Vidal, *Ius Canonicum,* 7 vols. in 9, Vol. V, *Ius Matrimoniale,* 2. ed., Romae: Apud Aedes Universitatis Gregorianae, 1928.

Whalen, Donald, *The Value of Testimonial Evidence in Matrimonial*

Procedure, The Catholic University of America, Canon Law Studies, n. 99, Washington: The Catholic University of America, 1935.

Periodicals

American Ecclesiastical Review, Philadelphia, 1889—
Apollinaris Commentarium Iuridico-Canonicum, Romae, 1928—
Archiv für katholisches Kircherecht Vol. I-VI, (1857-1861), Innsbruck; Vols. VI—(1862—), Mainz.
Irish Ecclesiastical Record, Dublin, 1864—
Ius Pontificium, Romae, 1921—
L'Ami du Clergé, Paris, 1878—
Michigan Law Review, Ann Arbor, 1903—
Monitore Ecclesiastico, Il, Romae, 1876—
Revue d'Histoire et de Litterature Religieuses, Paris, 1896-1907, 1910-1922.
Theologisch-pracktische Quartalschrift, Linz, 1832—
University of Pennsylvania Law Review, Philadelphia, 1852—

Principal Articles

Fink, P., "Über das Ehehindernis des bestehenden Ehebandes"—*Theologisch-praktische Quartalschrift,* LXXXVIII (1935), 809-815.
Lehmkuhl, Aug., "Wiederverheiratung nach längerem Vermisstsein des totgeglaubten Gatten"—*Theologisch-praktische Quartalschrift,* LXX (1917), 113-117.
Haring, Johann, "Eheabschluss ohne sicheren Todesnachweis des engegenstehenden Gatten"—*Theologisch-praktische Quartalschrift,* LXXXVI (1933), 376-378.
Hilling, N., "Kriegsverschollenheit und Eheschliessung"—*Archiv für katholisches Kirchenrecht,* XCV (1915), 160-163.
Schaaf, Valentine, "Proof of Death of Husband or Wife"—*American Ecclesiastical Review,* LXXXIX (1933), 282-286.
Schlenz, Johann, "Wiedervereheliehung auf Grund der Todeserklärung des anderen Ehegatten infolge Verschollenheit, mit besonder Berücksichtigung der Kriegsverschollenheit"—*Archiv für katholisches Kirchenrecht,* XCVIII (1918), 52-70, 215-222, 381-397, 549-560; CIV (1924), 206-223.
H.E.S., "Judicial Presumptions Respecting Irregular Marriage"—*University of Pennsylvania Law Review,* LXXXII (1933-1934), 508-515.
"Marriage—Validity—Disappearance of First Husband"—*Michigan Law Review,* VI (1908), 513-514.

Abbreviations

AAS—Acta Apostolicae Sedis.
AKKR—Archiv für katholisches Kirchenrecht.
AER—American Ecclesiastical Review.

ASS—Acta Sanctae Sedis.
Fontes—Codicis Iuris Canonici Fontes.
MGH—Monumenta Germaniae Historica.
MPG—Migne, *Patrologia, Series Graeca.*
MPL—Migne, *Patrologia, Series Latina.*
TPQ—Theologisch-praktisch Quartalschrift.

BIOGRAPHICAL NOTE

Patrick W. Rice was born on January 10, 1907, in New York City. After completing his high school course at St. Mary of the Mount High School, Pittsburgh, Pa., he matriculated at Duquesne University, Pittsburgh, Pa., and received the degree of Bachelor of Arts from this institution in 1927. His theological studies were made at St. Vincent Seminary, Latrobe, Pa., which he attended from 1927 to 1931. He was ordained to the priesthood on June 7, 1931. The next six years he spent in parish work in the Diocese of Pittsburgh. In September, 1937, he entered the School of Canon Law at the Catholic University of America, where he received the degree of the Baccalaureate in Canon Law in June, 1938, and the degree of the Licentiate in Canon Law in June, 1939.

ALPHABETICAL INDEX

Abbas Antiquus, 24.
Absence of spouse, 9, 27, 32, 84, 123.
Administrative procedure,
  general features of, 44.
  in proof of death, 40.
  terminology, 49.
Adua, battle of, 35, 93.
Advanced age, 87.
Alexander III,
  decretal letter of, 23.
  and *copula* theory, 20.
Anselm of Lucca, 17.
Appeal, 49, 52.
Aquinas, St. Thomas, 18.
Background of missing person, 85.
Bad faith, 116, 119.
Baltimore, Second Plenary Council of, 30, 58.
Bandinelli, Roland, 19.
Basil, St., 11.
Bigamy, 112.
Bond of marriage, 51.
Burchard, 16.
Captivity, 10, 21, 31.
Certificate of death, 31, 32, 55, 61, 62, 63, 64.
Certitude of death, 18, 21, 22, 23, 27, 41. cf. moral certitude.
Certum nuncium, 22.
Civil law, 121, 128.
Clement III, decretal letter of, 21, 31.
Collectio LXXIV Titulorum, 17.
Common opinion, 25, 97.
Competence, 48, 50.
Compiègne, Council of, 15, 16, 18.
Convalidation of marriage,
  in Canon law, 113.
  in the natural law, 115.
  in American civil law, 127.
Copula theory, 19.
Correspondence, cessation of, 88.
Counsellor, 51.
Crime, impediment of, 109, 114.
Cum alias, 30.
Death, in danger of, 58.
Debitum coniugale, 21, 118.
Decision of Ordinary, 107.
Declaration of death,
  by civil authorities, 65, 127.
  by ecclesiastical authorities, 108.
  by military authorities, 66.
Defensor vinculi, 50, 52.
Dionysio-Hadriana, Collectio, 16.
Disappearance, reasons for, 85.
Documentary process of canon 1990, 52, 114.
Documents, 60-64.
Doubt of first spouse's death, 21, 22, 33, 115-120.
Eye-witnesses, 56, 71, 73.
Gratian, 17.
Good faith, 33, 116, 118, 124.
Gregory IX, Decretals of, 21.
Health, 87.
Holy Office,
  instruction of 1670, 30.
  instruction of 1822, 33
  instruction of 1868, 34, 41, 50.
Hostiensis, 24.
Hugh of St. Victor, 18.
Innocent I, decretal letter of, 12, 17.
Innocent III, decretal letter of, 22.
Indissolubility of marriage, 2.
Infidel, when missing person is an, 59.
Instructio Austriaca, 29.
Interrogatories, 69, 73, 79.
Investigation,
  additional required, 107.
  necessity of thorough, 82.
Ivo of Chartres, 17.
Judges, number of, 51.
Judicial procedure, 44, 51, 53.

Legitimacy, 23, 112.
Leo I, St., decretal letter of, 12, 16.
Ligamen, impediment of, 1.
Lombard, Peter, 18.
Lucius III, decretal letter of, 21, 31.
Matrimonium ratum et non consummatum, 3, 111.
Messina and Reggio, earthquake of, 35, 91.
Metropolitan, 49.
Missing soldiers, 10, 63, 92.
Moral certitude, 23, 106, 107.
  cf. certitude.
News of a missing person, 87.
Notary, 47, 51.
Nullity cases, 114.
Oath,
  required, 69.
  suppletory, 79.
Officialis, 48, 50.
Ordinary as administrator, 48.
Panormitanus, 25.
Pastor's obligation to refer case to Ordinary, 53.
Pauline privilege, 59, 111.
Penitentials, 14-16.
Polygamy, 1.
Preliminary investigation of marriage, 4, 54.
Presumptions in general, 82.
Presumption of death,
  first permitted, 32.
  cases of, 98.
  rules for establishing, 35, 81, 84.
  in Roman law, 9.
  in American civil law, 122.
  in French civil law, 129.
  in German civil law, 128.
  in Italian civil law, 129.
Privilegium fidei, 3, 59.
Promoter of justice, 52.
Proof of death, 5.
Propagation of the Faith,
  instruction of 1792, 33.
  instruction of 1883, 35.
Putative marriages, 23, 112.
Recourse to the Holy See, 49, 107, 108.
Regino of Prüm, 16.
Return of missing spouse, 12, 111.
Rota, Sacred, 49.
Rufinus, 18.
Sanchez, 24.
Second marriages, 4.
Sentence, 52.
Shipwreck, 88.
Status liber, proof of, 4.
Summary procedure, 44, 45.
Tempus suspectum, 78.
Testimony,
  adminicular, 74, 78.
  of acquaintances, 73.
  evaluation of, 70.
  of relatives, 68, 72.
  of surviving spouse, 71.
  cf. witnesses.
Theodore, penitential of, 14.
Trent, Council of, 2, 26.
Trullo, Council of, 11.
Unity of marriage, 1, 43.
Use of marriage, when death of first spouse is doubtful, 118.
Verberies, Council of, 15, 16.
Vicar-general, 48.
Voluntary jurisdiction, 46.
Witness, one, 24, 73.
Witnesses,
  credibility of, 72.
  eye-, 56, 71, 73.
  in general, 67.
  hearsay, 77.
  in missionary countries, 73.
  qualified, 70.
War and persecution, 90.

CANON LAW STUDIES

1. Freriks, Rev. Celestine A., C.PP.S., J.C.D., Religious Congregations in Their External Relations, 121 pp., 1916.
2. Galliher, Rev. Daniel M., O.P., J.C.D., Canonical Elections, 117 pp., 1917.
3. Borkowski, Rev. Aurelius L., O.F.M., J.C.D., De Confraternitatibus Ecclesiasticis, 136 pp., 1918.
4. Castillo, Rev. Cayo, J.C.D., Disertacion Historico-Canonica sobre la Potestad del Cabildo en Sede Vacante o Impedida del Vicario Capitular, 99 pp., 1919 (1918).
5. Kubelbeck, Rev. William J., S.T.B., J.C.D., The Sacred Pentitentiaria and Its Relations to Faculties of Ordinaries and Priests, 129 pp., 1918.
6. Petrovits, Rev. Joseph J.C., S.T.D., J.C.D., The New Church Law On Matrimony, X-461 pp., 1919.
7. Hickey, Rev. John J., S.T.B., J.C.D., Irregularities and Simple Impediments in the New Code of Canon Law, 100 pp., 120.
8. Klekotka, Rev. Peter J., S.T.B., J.C.D., Diocesan Consultors, 179 pp., 1920.
9. Wanenmacher, Rev. Francis, J.C.D., The Evidence in Ecclesiastical Procedure Affecting the Marriage Bond, 1920 (Printed 1935).
10. Golden, Rev. Henry Francis, J.C.D., Parochial Benefices in the New Code, IV-119 pp., 1921 (Printed 1925).
11. Koudelka, Rev. Charles J., J.C.D., Pastors, Their Rights and Duties According to the New Code of Canon Law, 211 pp., 1921.
12. Melo, Rev. Antonius, O.F.M., J.C.D., De Exemptione Regularium, X-188 pp., 1921.
13. Schaaf, Rev. Valentine Theodore, O.F.M., S.T.B., J.C.D., The Cloister, X-180 pp., 1921.
14. Burke, Rev. Thomas Joseph, S.T.D., J.C.D., Competence in Ecclesiastical Tribunals, IV-117 pp., 1922.
15. Leech, Rev. George Leo, J.C.D., A Comparative Study of the Constitution, "Apostolicae Sedis" and the "Codex Juris Canonici," 179 pp., 1922.
16. Motry, Rev. Hubert Louis, S.T.D., J.C.D., Diocesan Faculties According to the Code of Canon Law, II-167 pp., 1922.
17. Murphy, Rev. George Lawrence, J.C.D., Delinquencies and Penalties in the Administration and Reception of the Sacraments, IV-121 pp., 1923.
18. O'Reilly, Rev. John Anthony, S.T.B., J.C.D., Ecclesiastical Sepulture in the New Code of Canon Law, II-129 pp., 1923.

19. Michàlicka, Rev. Wenceslas Cyrill, O.S.B., J.C.D., Judicial Procedure in Dismissal of Clerical Exempt Religious, 107 pp., 1923.
20. Dargin, Rev. Edward Vincent, S.T.B., J.C.D., Reserved Cases According to the Code of Canon Law, IV-103, pp., 1924.
21. Godfrey, Rev. John A., S.T.B., J.C.D., The Right of Patronage According to the Code of Canon Law, 153 pp., 1924.
22. Hagedorn, Rev. Francis Edward, J.C.D., General Legislation on Indulgences, II-154 pp., 1924.
23. King, Rev. James Ignatius, J.C.D., The Administration of the Sacraments to Dying Non-Catholics, V-141 pp., 1924.
24. Winslow, Rev. Francis Joseph, A.F.M., J.C.D., Vicars and Prefects Apostolic, IV-149 pp., 1924.
25. Correa, Rev. Jose Servelion, S.T.L., J.C.D., La Potestad Legislativa de la Iglesia Catolica, IV-127 pp., 1925.
26. Dugan, Rev. Henry Francis, A.M., J.C.D., The Judiciary Department of the Diocesan Curia, 87 pp., 1925.
27. Keller, Rev. Charles Frederick, S.T.B., J.C.D., Mass Stipends, 167 pp., 1925.
28. Paschang, Rev. John Linus, J.C.D., The Sacramentals According to the Code of Canon Law, 129 pp., 1925.
29. Pointek, Rev. Cyrillus, O.F.M., S.T.B., J.C.D., De Indulto Exclaustrationis necnon Saecularizationis, XIII-289 pp., 1925.
30. Kearney, Rev. Richard Joseph, S.T.B., J.C.D., Sponsors at Baptism According to the Code of Canon Law, IV-127 pp., 1925.
31. Bartlett, Rev. Chester Joseph, A.M., LL.B., J.C.D., The Tenure of Parochial Property in the United States of America, V-108 pp., 1926.
32. Kilker, Rev. Adrian Jerome, J.C.D., Extreme Unction, V-425 pp., 1926.
33. McCormick, Rev. Robert Emmett, J.C.D., Confessors of Religious, VIII-266 pp., 1926.
34. Miller, Rev. Newton Thomas, J.C.D., Founded Masses According to the Code of Canon Law, VII-93 pp., 1926.
35. Roelker, Rev. Edward G., S.T.D., J.C.D., Principles of Privilege According to the Code of Canon Law, XI-166 pp., 1926.
36. Bakalarczyk, Rev. Richardus, M.I.C., J.U.D., De Novitiatu, VIII-208 pp., 1927.
37. Pizzuti, Rev. Lawrence, O.F.M., J.U.L., De Parochis Religiosis, 1927. (Not printed).
38. Bliley, Rev. Nicholas Martin, O.S.B., J.C.D., Altars According to the Code of Canon Law, XIX-132 pp., 1927.
39. Brown, Mr. Brendan Francis, A.B. LL.M., J.U.D., The Canonical Juristic Personality with Special Reference to Its Status in the United States of America, V-212 pp., 1927.

40. Cavanaugh, Rev. William Thomas, C.P., J.U.D., The Reservation of the Blessed Sacrament, VIII-101 pp., 1927.
41. Doheny, Rev. William J., C.S.C., A.B., J.U.D., Church Property: Modes of Acquisition, X-118 pp., 1927.
42. Feldhaus, Rev. Aloysius H., C.PP.S., J.C.D., Oratories, IX-141 pp., 1927.
43. Kelly, Rev. James Patrick, A.B., J.C.D., The Jurisdiction of the Simple Confessor, X-208 pp., 1927.
44. Neuberger, Rev. Nicholas J., J.C.D., Canon 6 or the Relation of the Codex Juris Canonici to the Preceding Legislation, V-95 pp., 1927.
45. O'Keefe, Rev. Gerald Michael, J.C.D., Matrimonial Dispensations, Powers of Bishops, Priests and Confessors, VIII-232 pp., 1927.
46. Quigley, Rev. Joseph A.M., A.B., J.C.B., Condemned Societies, 139 pp., 1927.
47. Zaplotnik, Rev. Johannes Leo, J.C.D., De Vicariis Foraneis, X-142 pp., 1927.
48. Duskie, Rev. John Aloysius, A.B., J.C.D., The Canonical Status of the Orientals in the United States, VIII-196 pp., 1928.
49. Hyland, Rev. Francis Edward, J.C.D., Excommunication, Its Nature, Historical Development and Effects, VIII-181 pp., 1928.
50. Reinmann, Rev. Gerald Joseph, O.M.C., J.C.D., The Third Order Secular of Saint Francis, 201 pp., 1928.
51. Schenk, Rev. Francis J., J.C.D., The Matrimonial Impediments of Mixed Religion and Disparity of Cult, XVI-318 pp., 1929.
52. Coady, Rev. John Joseph, S.T.D., J.U.D., A.M., The Appointment of Pastors, VIII-150 pp., 1929.
53. Kay, Rev. Thomas Henry, J.C.D., Competence in Matrimonial Procedure, VIII-164 pp., 1929.
54. Turner, Rev. Sidney Joseph, C.P., J.U.D., The Vow of Poverty, XLIX-217 pp., 1929.
55. Kearney, Rev. Raymond, A., A.B., S.T.D., J.C.D., The Principles, of Delegation, VII-149 pp., 1929.
56. Conran, Rev. Edward James, A.B., J.C.D., The Interdict, V-163 pp., 1930.
57. O'Neil, Rev. William H., J.C.D., Papal Rescripts of Favor, VII-218 pp., 1930.
58. Bastnagel, Rev. Clement Vincent, J.U.D., The Appointment of Parochial Adjutants and Assistants, XV-257 pp., 1930.
59. Ferry, Rev. William A., A.B., J.C.D., Stole Fees, V-135 pp., 1930.
60. Costello, Rev. John Michael, A.B., J.C.D., Domicile and Quasi-domicile, VII-201 pp., 1930.
61. Kremer, Rev. Michael Nicholas, A.B., S.T.B., J.C.D., Church Support in the United States, VI-1930.

62. Angulo, Rev. Luis, C.M., J.C.D., Legislation de la Iglesia sobre la intencion en la application de la Santa Misa, VII-104 pp., 1931.
63. Frey, Rev. Wolfgang Norbert, O.S.B., A.B., J.C.D., The Act of Religious Profession, VIII-174 pp., 1931.
64. Roberts, Rev. James Brendan, A.B., J.C.D., The Banns of Marriage, XIV-140 pp., 1931.
65. Ryder, Rev. Raymond Aloysius, A.B., J.C.D., Simony, IX-151 pp., 1931.
66. Campagna, Rev. Angelo, Ph.D., J.U.D., Il Vicario Generale del Vescovo, VII-205 pp., 1931.
67. Cox, Rev. Joseph Godfrey, A.B., J.C.D., The Administration of Seminaries, VI-124 pp., 1931.
68. Gregory, Rev. Donald J., J.U.D., The Pauline Privilege, XV-165 pp., 1931.
69. Donohue, Rev. John F., J.C.D., The Impediment of Crime, VII-110 pp., 1931.
70. Dooley, Rev. Eugene A., O.M.I., J.C.D., Church Law On Sacred Relics, IX-143 pp., 1931.
71. Orth, Rev. Raymond Clement, O.M.C., J.C.D., The Approbation of Religious Institutes, 171 pp., 1931.
72. Pernicone, Rev. Joseph M., A.B., J.C.D., The Ecclesiastical Prohibition of Books, XII-267 pp., 1932.
73. Clinton, Rev. Connell, A.B., J.C.D., The Paschal Precept, IX-108 pp., 1932.
74. Donnelly, Rev. Francis B., A.M., S.T.L., J.C.D., The Diocesan Synod, VIII-125 pp., 1932.
75. Torrente, Rev. Camilo, C.M.F., J.C.D., Las Processiones Sagradas, V-145 pp., 1932.
76. Murphy, Rev. Edwin J., C.PP.S., J.C.D., Suspension Ex Informata Conscientia, XI-122, pp., 1932.
77. Mackenzie, Rev. Eric F., A.M., S.T.L., J.C.D., The Delict of Heresy in its Commission Penalization, Absolution, VII-124 pp., 1932.
78. Lyons Rev. Avitus E., S.T.B., J.C.D., The Collegiate Tribunal of First Instance, XI-147 pp., 1932.
79. Connolly, Rev. Thomas A., J.C.D., Appeals, XI-195 pp., 1932.
80. Sangmeister, Rev. Joseph V., A.B., J.C.D., Force and Fear as Precluding Matrimonial Consent, V-211 pp., 1932.
81. Jaeger, Rev. Leo A., A.B., J.C.D., The Administration of Vacant and Quasi-vacant Episcopal Sees in the United States, IX-229 pp., 1932.
82. Rimlinger, Rev. Herbert T., J.C.D., Error Invalidating Matrimonial Consent, VII-79 pp., 1932.
83. Barrett, Rev. John D.M., S.S., J.C.D., A Comparative Study of the Third Plenary Council of Baltimore and the Code, IX-221 pp., 1932.

84. Carberry, Rev. John J., Ph.D., S.T.D., J.C.D., The Juridical Form of Marriage, X-177 pp., 1934.
85. Dolan, Rev. John L., A.B., J.C.D., The Defensor Vinculi, XII-157 pp., 1934.
86. Hannan, Rev. Jerome D., A.M., S.T.D., LL.B., J.C.D., The Canon Law of Wills, IX-517 pp., 1934.
87. Lemieux, Rev. Delisle A., A.M., J.C.D., The Sentence in Ecclesiastical Procedure, IX-131 pp., 1934.
88. O'Rourke, Rev. James J., A.B., J.C.D., Parish Registers, VII-109 pp., 1934.
89. Timlin, Rev. Bartholomew, O.F.M., A.M., J.C.D., Conditional Matrimonial Consent, X-381 pp., 1934.
90. Wahl, Rev. Francis X., A.B., J.C.D., The Matrimonial Impediments of Consanguinity and Affinity, VI-125 pp., 1934.
91. White, Rev. Robert J., A.B., LL.B., S.T.B., J.C.D., Canonical Ante-Nuptial Promises and the Civil Law, VI-152 pp., 1934.
92. Herrera, Rev. Antonio Parra, O.C.D., J.C.D., Legislation Ecclesiastica sobra el Ayuno y la Abstinencia, XI-191 pp., 1935.
93. Kennedy, Rev. Edwin J., J.C.D., The Special Matrimonial Process in Cases of Evident Nullity, X-165 pp., 1935.
94. Manning, Rev. John J., A.B., J.C.D., Presumption of Law in Matrimonial Procedure, XI-111 pp., 1935.
95. Moeder, Rev. John M., J.C.D., The Proper Bishop for Ordination and Dismissorial Letters, VII-135 pp., 1935.
96. O'Mara, Rev. William A., A.B., J.C.D., Canonical Causes For Matrimonial Dispensations, IX-155 pp., 1935.
97. Reilly, Rev. Peter, J.C.D., Residence of Pastors, IX-81 pp., 1935.
98. Smith, Rev. Mariner T., O.P., S.T.L., J.C.D., The Penal Law For Religious, VII-169 pp., 1935.
99. Whalen, Rev. Donald W., A.M., J.C.D., The Value of Testimonial Evidence in Matrimonial Procedure, XIII-297 pp., 1935.
100. Cleary, Rev. Joseph F., J.C.D., Canonical Limitations on the Alienation of Church Property, VIII-141 pp., 1936.
101. Glynn, Rev. John C., J.C.D., The Promoter of Justice, XX-337 pp., 1936.
102. Brennan, Rev. James H., S.S., A.M., S.T.B., J.C.D., The Simple Convalidation of Marriage, VI-135 pp, 1937.
103. Brunini, Rev. Joseph Bernard, J.C.D., The Clerical Obligations of Canons, 139 and 142, X-121 pp., 1937.
104. Connor, Rev. Maurice, A.B., J.C.D., The Administrative Removal of Pastors, VIII-159 pp., 1937.
105. Guilfoyle, Rev. Merlin Joseph, J.C.D., Custom, XI-144 pp., 1937.
106. Hughes, Rev. James Austin, A.B., A.M., J.C.D., Witnesses in Criminal Trials of Clerics, IX-140 pp., 1937.

107. Jansen, Rev. Raymond J., A.B., S.T.L., J.C.D., Canonical Provisions for Catechetical Instruction, VII-153 pp., 1937.
108. Kealy, Rev. John James, A.B., J.C.D,, The Introductory Libellus in Church Court Procedure, XI-121 pp., 1937.
109. McManus, Rev. James Edward, C.SS.R., J.C.D., The Administration of Temporal Goods in Religious Institutes, XVI-196 pp., 1937.
110. Moriarity, Rev. Eugene James, J.C.D., Oaths in Ecclesiastical Courts, X-115 pp., 1937.
111. Rainer, Rev. Eligius George, C.SS.R., J.C.D., Suspension of Clerics, XVII-249 pp., 1937.
112. Reilly, Rev. Thomas F., C.SS.R., J.C.D., Visitation of Religious, VI-195 pp., 1938.
113. Moriarty, Rev. Francis E., C.SS.R., J.C.D., The Extraordinary Absolution from Censures, XV-334 pp., 1938.
114. Connolly, Rev. Nicholas P., J.C.D., The Canonical Erection of Parishes, X-132 pp., 1938.
115. Donovan, Rev. James Joseph, J.C.D., The Pastor's Obligation in Prenuptial Investigation, XII-322 pp., 1938.
116. Harrigan, Rev. Robert J., M.A., S.T.B., J.C.D., The Radical Sanation of Invalid Marriages, VIII-208 pp., 1938.
117. Boffa, Rev. Conrad Humbert, J.C.D., Canonical Provisions for Catholic Schools, X-211 pp., 1939.
118. Parsons, Rev. Anscar John, O.M. Cap., J.C.D., Canonical Elections, XII-236 pp., 1939.
119. Reilly, Rev. Edward Michael, A.B., J.C.D., The General Norms ot Dispensation, X-156 pp., 1939.
120. Ryan, Rev. Gerald Aloysius, A.B., J.C.D., Principles of Episcopal Jurisdiction, XII-172 pp., 1939.
121. Burton, Rev. Francis James, C.S.C., A.B., J.C.L., A Commentary on Canon 1125.
122. Miaskiewicz, Rev. Francis Sigismund, J.C.L., Supplied Jurisdiction According to Canon 209.
123. Rice, Rev. Patrick William, A. B., J.C.L., Proof of Death in Prenuptial Investigation.

www.ingramcontent.com/pod-product-compliance
Lightning Source LLC
LaVergne TN
LVHW050224080826
844660LV00012B/464

* 9 7 8 0 8 1 3 2 2 3 1 2 4 *